"Don't pick up this book—unless you're willing to get hooked! It's compelling, practical, and full of creative ideas. Any catechist reading it can expect to feel confident and prepared to use stories to teach as Jesus did.

"Janaan and Carl, pre-eminent catechists and storytellers, not only show readers how to use the art of storytelling to catechize children, they also catechize us as well. As I read through their life stories, I was inspired to recapture some of my own life story and to follow their footsteps in reflecting on how to live a richer, more balanced Christian life. I wanted to savor and save each story whether from Janaan and Carl's own experience, stories told about other people, or the treasurehouse of stories shared from other popular literature."

Jean Marie Hiesberger
Editor, *FaithWorks* catechetical newsletter

"Janaan Manternach and Carl Pfeifer have done it again! They have given us practical suggestions on ways to enrich our faith sharing through storytelling. Once you have walked through these stories with them, you will no longer dismiss the list of 'suggested stories' in your teacher's manual to enhance your weekly lesson. They will take their rightful and long overdue place in bringing the good news to life.

"This delightful book of stories from life and literature is a welcome resource for both DREs and catechists. *How Creative Catechists Use Stories* is a must for your new millennium library."

Gail Thomas McKenna
Author, *Models and Trends in Religious Education*

"Madeline L'Engle wrote, 'Jesus was not a theologian. He was God who told stories.' *How Creative Catechists Use Stories* helps us follow Jesus' example, showing us how to successfully touch this generation of postmodern children with the pivotal message of the gospel: Jesus loves me; Jesus loves you.

"Manternach and Pfeifer's book teaches, but more importantly, it's a storybook. Propositions are presented; I learn, but I learn softly through story. These stories are sneaky! They make me think, and then think again. These talented religious educators have written a stay-on-my-shelf book that I can use both with volunteer teachers and with the children God has given me to teach."

Marlene LeFever
Editor, *Teacher Touch*
Director of Church relations, Cook Communications Ministries

How Creative Catechists Use Stories

Janaan Manternach and Carl J. Pfeifer

TWENTY-THIRD PUBLICATIONS
BAYARD Mystic, CT 06355

Credits

Permission granted for stories used from the *Sower's Seeds* series, by Brian Cavanaugh, as follows: *The Sower's Seeds*, copyright ©1990; *More Sower's Seeds: Second Planting*, copyright ©1992; *Fresh Packet of Sower's Seeds: Third Planting*, copyright ©1994; *Sower's Seeds Aplenty: Fourth Planting*, copyright ©1996. All published by Paulist Press, Mahwah, NJ.

With Love at Christmas, by Mem Fox, reprinted with permission of Jenny Darling & Associates. Published by Abingdon Press, Nashville, TN; copyright ©1989.

Excerpts from *The Catholic Source Book*, by Peter Klein, reprinted with permission of Harcourt, Inc. Published by Brown-ROA, Dubuque, IA; copyright ©2000.

Marvin K. Mooney Will You Please Go Now!, by Dr. Seuss. TM & copyright ©1972 by Dr. Seuss Enterprises, L.P. Reprinted by permission of Random House Children's Books, a division of Random House, Inc.

Stepka and the Magic Fire, by Dorothy VanWoerkom. Reprinted with permission of John W. VanWoerkom. Published by Concordia Publishing House, St. Louis, MO; copyright ©1974.

Twenty-Third Publications/ Bayard
185 Willow Street
P.O. Box 180
Mystic, CT 06355
(860) 536-2611
(800) 321-0411

© Copyright 2000 Janaan Manternach and Carl J. Pfeifer. All rights reserved. No part of this publication may be reproduced in any manner without prior written permission of the publisher. Write to the Permissions Editor.

ISBN:1-58595-112-9
Library of Congress Catalog Card Number: 00-134395
Printed in the U.S.A.

Dedication

To Anita V. Manternach
who prayed this book to completion
and is our Mother and Friend.

Contents

1. Teaching with Story — 1
2. Christians in Community — 8
3. Seeing Others as Equal & Worthwhile — 14
4. Treating Others with Compassion & Justice — 20
5. Making Daily Decisions through Moral Choices — 27
6. Beginning Anew through Forgiveness & Reconciliation — 33
7. God's Presence Sustains Us — 40
8. Living the Sabbath with Rest & Presence — 46
9. Advent: Preparing for Christ's Coming — 52
10. Christmas: Celebrating the Incarnation — 58
11. Lent: Observing with Prayer, Fasting, & Almsgiving — 66
12. Easter: Celebrating Christ's Resurrection — 74
13. Jesus Is Central to Our Lives as Christians — 82

Bibliography — 89

1

Teaching with Story

Story is one of the most powerful resources available to us for teaching religion. Yet this marvelous tool is too seldom used by catechists and religion teachers. This book is an attempt to change that.

When we speak to religion teachers and catechists about the use of story in their classes, we realize that there is a great deal of interest in and enthusiasm for this topic. But soon, it often seems, both the interest and enthusiasm wane and the desire to use story is eclipsed by the other "have-to-dos" of teaching. While many religion textbooks suggest and include stories from children's literature in their lesson plans, some catechists and religion teachers skip over them in order to devote more time to what they believe is most important.

Why Story Is Important
Story connects with the whole of life; Janaan's first professor of theology taught her about this. She used children's literature as a major resource in teaching theology, especially *The World of Pooh*, by A.A. Milne. (See the Bibliography at the end of this book for publisher information on this and every other book mentioned here.) The professor's rationale was that "the more we get into story, the more we get into life, and the more we get into life, the more we get into God." Indeed, Janaan owes her deep and abiding interest in story to this woman.

Children's literature deals with every aspect of the human and divine. It does so unabashedly, perceptively, and often in a way that challenges the reader to consider a more loving, more careful, and wiser way to live. Here is an example. During our goddaughter Angela's adolescence, Janaan had her read books that she was thinking of adding to bibliographies. She wanted Angela to read them thoughtfully and to write a few paragraphs about each one, saying whether or not they had an impact on her and also, if she would recommend the books to other people her age. To assure that she took the task seriously, Janaan paid her for the time it took to read and write a review.

From the time she was twelve until she was sixteen, Angela read many books and evaluated them for Janaan. One of the books she read was *Go Ask Alice* (author anonymous). It's a true story that grew out of a diary kept by Alice. The following is what Angela wrote after she read the book:

> *Go Ask Alice* had a very profound impact on me. The most amazing thing, for me, about the story is that "Alice" got mixed

up in drugs by a stupid game, in which she is completely innocent. The scary part about that is that she's not the only person who has put drugs into her body and not known until afterwards.

This book is definitely something that should be read by all teenagers. (Probably a better "girl" book than a "guy" book.) Anyone who has done drugs or even thought about it should especially read this book. If you haven't, after reading this you won't want to do drugs for sure. *Go Ask Alice* really opens your eyes to all the harm that drugs can have on your body, and it could turn you away from them. At least it did for me. As they say in the book, "After you've had it, there isn't even life without drugs." (That was an excerpt from one of Alice's diary entries).

Story Instructs

Besides connecting to the whole of life, story instructs. G. K. Chesterton, in the chapter titled "The Ethics of Elfland" in his book *Orthodoxy*, said that "the most important things he learned, he learned from fairy tales."

Yuko Sato, the figure skater from Japan, first learned English by reading children's books. Barbara Meister Vitale, in the introduction to her book, *Unicorns Are Real*, writes:

> I was a child with a learning disability, labeled "slow" for my first four years of school. I was unable to read until I was twelve years old. Even today I have severe language reversals.
>
> I was lucky! When I was in the fifth grade, a wonderful teacher found me and believed in me. She helped me believe in myself! She taught me that my way of thinking was not just different but special! And she taught me to read! She didn't hand me a reading book or instruct me in a reading group; instead, she let me pick out my own books. I picked Grimm's Fairy Tales. They were too hard but she never let me know it. We learned the words one by one until I could read a whole story.

A story that reveals the power of instruction in literature is "Even Teacups Talk," in *Sower's Seeds of Encouragement: Fifth Planting* (Paulist Press).

Story Lodges Itself in the Memory

Another value that story has is that it lodges itself in the memory and thereby empowers. This is illustrated in "Telling One's Own Story," (anonymous), in *The Sower's Seeds*, by Brian Cavanaugh.

> When the great Rabbi Israel Baal Shem-Tov saw misfortune threatening the Jews, it was his custom to go into a certain part of the forest to meditate. There he would light a fire, say a prayer, and a miracle would be accomplished and the misfortune averted.
>
> Later, when his disciple, the celebrated Magid of Mezritch, had occasion, for the same reason, to say the prayer, he would go to the same place in the forest and say: "Master of the Universe, listen! I do not know how to light the fire, but I am still able to say the prayer." And, again, a miracle would be accomplished.
>
> Still later, Rabbi Moshe-Leib of Sasov, in order to save his people once more, would go into the forest and say: "I do not know how to light the fire, I do not know the prayer, but I know the place, and this must be sufficient." Once again, a miracle.
>
> Then it fell to Rabbi Israel of Rizhyn to

overcome misfortune. Sitting in his armchair, his head in his hands, he spoke to God: "I am unable to light the fire and I do not know the prayer; I cannot even find the place in the forest. All I can do is tell the story, and this must be sufficient." And it was sufficient.

Story Heals
Story makes us laugh, cry, wonder, imagine. It also heals. For example: when our godchildren's parents chose to separate and eventually divorce, Miguel was seven. He hurt so badly at times, he didn't know what to do with the pain. One afternoon he was feeling so sad that he couldn't sit still, he wasn't hungry, and he didn't want to play. So Janaan sat with him on our front stoop and they were mostly not saying anything. But then Janaan asked, "Mig, if you had one wish, what would it be?"

He looked at Janaan, his eyes filled with tears and, with all his heart, he said, "I wish it would just go away." Janaan didn't know what to say back but while she was hurting with him, she said, "Mig, a really great man called Dr. Seuss may have understood what you're feeling because he wrote a book about what you're wishing. Let me get the book and we'll read it together."

The book is *Marvin K. Mooney Will You Please Go Now!*. The first part of the story goes like this:

The time has come.
The time is now.
Just go.
Go.
Go!
I don't care how.
You can go by foot.
You can go
by cow.
Marvin K. Mooney,
will you
please go now!
You can go
on skates
You can go
on skis.
You can go
in a hat.
But please go.
Please!
I don't care.
You can go
by bike.
You can go
on a Zike-Bike
if you like.
If you like
you can go
in an old blue shoe.
Just go, go, GO!
Please do, do, DO!
Marvin K. Mooney,
I don't care how.
Marvin K. Mooney
will you please
GO NOW!

By the time we finished reading the story, Miguel was laughing and feeling much better. It certainly didn't take away all his pain, but it healed enough.

Jesus Used Story
Perhaps the most important reason for using story is that Jesus, and the Hebrew prophets before him, taught chiefly through stories. Whenever Jesus taught or answered a question, he told a parable, a story. His intriguing, challenging stories have continued to touch people profoundly for some twenty centuries.

We continue, in the third millennium, to

ponder, probe, tell, act out, and live by his stories. He spoke of life's deepest mysteries in stories about housewives baking bread and farmers planting seed. In his stories are taxpayers, prostitutes, unjust judges, rich fools, birds, fig trees, servants and masters, the rich and the poor, the pious and the sinner, and wise and foolish virgins. Jesus was one of the best—if not the very best—of all teachers who use stories.

Recommended Readings
Story has the power to transform lives—our own and those of our students. It is good, therefore, to both read and read about stories. To read about story, we recommend:

Storytelling: Imagination and Faith, by William J. Bausch. This is both a book of stories and a book about storytelling. The introduction begins with the observation that the phrase, "Once upon a time" is no time and every time. It is the standard phrase that introduces us to other worlds and to our own world, that connects humanity to a common story and storyteller. That is why storytelling and story listening are so congenial, for, in one way or another, we are hearing about ourselves.

Chapter four, "Story and Imagination," in *The Art of Catechesis*, by Maureen Gallagher. Maureen makes a convincing case for the teaching value of stories and also shows how they clarify the truth, offer opportunities to laugh and cry, awaken spiritual awareness, heal wounds, build memory banks, and unite communities. She believes that, without story, "propositions about faith are dull and lifeless." And, that "stories are the tool of the catechist as a brush is the tool of a painter."

Books that Build Character, by William Kilpatrick and Suzanne M. Wolfe. The authors suggest that reading aloud may be one of the most important contributions parents can make toward developing good character in their children: "First, because stories can create an emotional attachment to goodness, a desire to do the right thing. Second, because stories provide a wealth of good examples—the kind of examples that are often missing from a child's day-to-day environment. Third, because stories familiarize children with the codes of conduct they need to know. Finally, because stories help to make sense out of life, help us to cast our own lives as stories. Unless this sense of meaning is acquired at an early age and reinforced as we grow older, there simply is no moral growth."

Gospel Light, by John Shea. John is an inveterate believer in the power of story and has spent his life looking at humanity, mystery, and grace through the perspective of story. In this book, he takes the Jesus stories and helps us, step-by-step, to understand them as tools of spiritual transformation. This is the best book on gospel stories that we have ever read.

Stories Affirm and Give Hope
Finally, filling children's minds and hearts with stories can affirm the gifts and talents they have and, also give them hope. An example of this kind of story is "Let the Music Out," (anonymous), from *More Sower's Seeds: Second Planting*, by Brian Cavanaugh.

> Three neighborhood boys, Salvator, Julio and Antonio, lived and played in Cremona, Italy, around the mid-1600s. Salvator had a beautiful tenor voice and Julio played the violin in accompaniment as they strolled the piazzas. Antonio also liked music and would have loved to sing along but his voice squeaked like a creaky door hinge. All the children made

fun of him whenever he tried to sing. Yet Antonio was not without talent. His most prized possession was the pocketknife his grandfather had given him. He was always whittling away on some piece of wood. In fact, Antonio made some very nice things with his whittling.

As the time for the annual festival approached, the houses and streets gradually became festooned with beautiful decorations for spring. Dressed in their finest clothes, people filled the streets. On festival day, Salvator and Julio planned to go to the cathedral where they would play and sing in the crowded plaza.

"Would you like to come with us?" they called to Antonio, who sat on his stoop whittling on a piece of wood. "Who cares if you can't sing. We'd like to have you come with us anyway."

"Sure, I'd like to come along," Antonio replied. "The festival is so much fun."

The three boys went off to the cathedral. As they walked along, Antonio kept thinking about their remark about his not being able to sing. It made him cry in his heart because he loved music as much as they did, even if his voice did squeak a little.

When they arrived at the plaza, Julio began to play the violin while Salvator sang with his melodious voice. People stopped to listen, and most of them left a coin or two for the shabbily dressed boys. An elderly man stepped out from the crowd. He complimented them and placed a shiny coin into Salvator's hand. He was quickly lost in the milling crowd.

Salvator opened his hand and gasped, "Look! It's a gold coin." He clenched it between his teeth to make sure. All three boys were excited and passed the coin back and forth, examining it. They all agreed it was a real gold piece.

"But he can well afford it," said Julio. "You know, he's the great Amati."

Antonio asked sheepishly, "And who is Amati? Why is he so great?"

Both boys laughed as they said, "You've never heard of Amati?"

"Of course he hasn't," said Julio. "He knows nothing about musicmakers. He has a squeaky voice and is just a whittler of wood." Julio went on, "For your information, Antonio, Amati happens to be a great violin-maker, probably the best in all of Italy or even the entire world, and he even lives here in our city."

As Antonio walked home that evening, his heart was very heavy. It seemed that he had been laughed at too often for his squeaky voice and his whittling. So, very early the next morning, Antonio left his home, carrying his precious whittling knife. His pockets were stuffed with some of the things he had made—a pretty bird, a flute, several statues and a small boat. He was determined to find the home of the great Amati.

Eventually Antonio found the house and gently knocked on the front door. When a servant opened it, the great master heard Antonio's squeaky voice and came to see what he wanted so early in the morning.

"I brought these for you to see, sir," replied Antonio, as he emptied his pockets of the assortment of items that he had carved. "I hope you will look at these and tell me if I have enough talent to learn how to make violins, too."

Amati carefully picked up and examined each piece, and invited Antonio into his house. "What is your name?" he asked.

"Antonio, sir," he squeaked.

"And why do you want to make violins," inquired Amati, now quite serious.

Impulsively Antonio blurted, "Because I love music, but I cannot sing with a voice that sounds like a squeaky door hinge. You heard how good my friends are yesterday in front of the cathedral. I, too, want to make music come alive."

Leaning forward and looking Antonio in the eyes, Amati said, "The thing that matters most is the song in the heart. There are many ways of making music—some people play the violin, others sing, still others paint wonderful pictures. Each help to add to the splendor of the world. You are a whittler, but your song shall be as noble as any."

These words made Antonio very happy, and he never forgot this message of hope. In a very short while, Antonio became a student of the great artist. Very early, every morning, he went to Amati's workshop, where he listened and learned and watched his teacher. After many years, there was not one secret about the making of a violin, with all of its seventy different parts, that he did not know. By the time he was twenty-two years old, his master allowed him to put his own name on a violin he had made.

For the rest of his life, Antonio Stradivari made violins—more than 1,100 of them—trying to make each one better and more beautiful than the one before. Anyone who owns a Stradivarius violin owns a treasure, a masterpiece of art.

We may not be able to sing, play, whittle or make a violin, but if we really want to, we will find a way to let the music out of our hearts and to praise God with it.

Give story a try. To begin, we recommend that you build one story per month into your lesson plan. That would amount to nine stories a year. In the chapters that follow, we will choose a theme and suggest stories that fit into that theme.

Note: Some of the books mentioned in *How Creative Catechists Use Stories* are now out of print. If you find this is so for a particular title you are seeking, try your local library to see if they have a copy. Most libraries have an intrastate loaning service, so that even if your library does not have a copy of a particular book, they may be able to get it for you from another branch.

For Your Reflection & Response

• Visit your local library and become acquainted with *The Horn Book Magazine* and *The Horn Book Guide*. They are great resources for keeping up-to-date on new children's and teen literature with reviews and symbols indicating the reviewer's pick of the best stories.

• At one of your faculty meetings share with each other favorite books from your childhood, or from reading to your children at home and/or in your classes.

• Take time to read *The Read-aloud Handbook*, by Jim Trelease. Be sure to get the latest copyrighted edition because he occasionally updates the section in the back titled "Treasury of Read-alouds."

2

Christians in Community

Community is a characteristic that has to be experienced before it is valued. It has to be witnessed before it is desired. We know this is true because we have experienced community again and again in our families, our parish, our neighborhood, and in schools.

A recent experience convinced us even more of the value of community. We were invited to be retreat masters for the yearly retreat of one of the local "Teams of Our Lady." This group meets regularly in Mount Vernon, Virginia, and four couples, a widow, and a chaplain make up this team. They have been together, with the exception of the chaplain, for seventeen years and have experienced births, illnesses, deaths, graduations, and weddings of their children, a remarriage of one of their members, the ordination to deacon of another, the births and baptisms of grandchildren, and a myriad of other good and bad times. Through it all they've gathered once a month for prayer, study, discussion, and dinner as well as for their yearly retreat.

There is a camaraderie among them that is palpable, a caring that is genuine, and a joy that is deep and inspiring. There is also an abiding sense that with the companionship and support of each other, "all will be well," to use the words of Julian of Norwich, no matter what happens.

As Carl and I were driving home from the retreat, we remarked to each other that it probably was the best thing we'd ever done. We also decided that we would say "Yes" in a heartbeat were they to invite us to present another retreat. But the more we talked about what had happened at the retreat we realized it wasn't what Carl and I had done so much as what being with the team had done for us. The team had welcomed us, included us in every part of the experience, shared stories of both the good and bad in their lives, past as well as present. They had prayed and celebrated with us. They had also listened to us, shown us respect and appreciation, and, more than anything else, they made us feel like one of their own. We found ourselves hungering for more experiences of community in our own lives and renewing our belief in its value.

What is profoundly true of community is that we need it because it embraces, supports, inspires, and challenges us all. It provides an environment in which people survive and thrive together, and in which a belief system and a faith tradition can take root and grow.

Creating Community in Religion Classes
During the years that Anna Thompson was coordinator of religious education at Holy Trinity Parish in Washington, DC, Carl and I were catechists in the parish program. Anna was genuinely interested in what we taught in our classes, but her main concern was that we create community with the children and young people in our classes. She encouraged eating a snack and talking together before we began any actual instruction. She told us again and again that the children were to see Christ in us, but we were also to see Christ in the children.

One of our first tasks was to learn the names of the children, and during subsequent classes to employ creative ways for getting to know each one. Respect and reverence for ourselves and each one of them were to be hallmarks of our endeavors. All these practices worked, and lasting friendships grew out of those years. Many of the young people in those classes went on to become catechists themselves, as well as become involved in other ministries, inspired, no doubt, by a sense of belonging to a community and responding to some of its needs. They liked what happened to them while they were with us, and what happened to others when they were with them.

A story that describes some of what happened to all of us during that time as we committed ourselves to seeing the divine in each other, is "The Rabbi's Gift," (anonymous), in *The Sower's Seeds*, by Brian Cavanaugh.

> There was a famous monastery which had fallen on hard times. Formerly its many buildings were filled with young monks and its big church resounded with the singing of the chant, but now it was nearly deserted. People no longer came there to be nourished by prayer. A handful of old monks shuffled through the cloisters and praised their God with heavy hearts.
>
> On the edge of the monastery woods, an old rabbi had built a little hut. He would come there from time to time to fast and pray. No one ever spoke with him, but whenever he appeared, the word would be passed from monk to monk: "The rabbi walks in the woods." And for as long as he was there the monks would feel sustained by his prayerful presence.
>
> One day the abbot decided to visit the rabbi and to open his heart to him. So after the morning eucharist, he set out through the woods. As he approached the hut, the abbot saw the rabbi standing in the doorway, his arms outstretched in welcome. It was as though he had been waiting there for some time. The two embraced like long-lost brothers. Then they stepped back and just stood there, smiling at one another with smiles their faces could hardly contain.
>
> After a while the rabbi motioned the abbot to enter. In the middle of the room was a wooden table with the Scriptures open on it. They sat there for a moment in the presence of the book. Then the rabbi began to cry. The abbot could not contain himself. He covered his face with his hands and began to cry, too. For the first time in his life, he cried his heart out. The two men sat there like lost children, filling the hut with their sobs and wetting the wood of the table with their tears.
>
> After the tears had ceased to flow and

all was quiet again, the rabbi lifted his head. "You and your brothers are serving God with heavy hearts," he said. "You have come to ask a teaching of me. I will give you this teaching but you can only repeat it once. After that, no one must say it again."

The rabbi looked straight at the abbot and said, "The messiah is among you." For awhile all was silent. Then the rabbi said, "Now you must go." The abbot left without a word and without looking back.

The next morning the abbot called his monks together in the chapter room. He told them he had received a teaching from "the rabbi who walks in the woods" and that this teaching was never again to be spoken aloud. Then he looked at each of his brothers and said, "The rabbi said that one of us is the messiah!"

The monks were startled by this. "What could it mean?" they asked themselves. "Is Brother John the messiah? Or Father Matthew? Or Brother Thomas? Am I the messiah? What could this mean?" They were all deeply puzzled by the rabbi's teaching. But no one ever mentioned it again.

As time went by, the monks began to treat one another with a very special reverence. There was a gentle, wholehearted, human quality about them now which was hard to describe but easy to notice. They lived with one another as men who had finally found something. But they prayed the Scriptures together as men who were always looking for something. Occasional visitors found themselves deeply moved by the life of these monks. Before long, people were coming from far and wide to be nourished by the prayer life of the monks, while young men were asking, once again, to become part of the community.

In those days the rabbi no longer walked in the woods. His hut had fallen into ruins. But somehow or other, the old monks who had taken his teaching to heart still felt sustained by his prayerful presence.

Creating Community through Partnership

The partnership aspect is another essential element in the creation of community. What flows from or is produced by the work that we do, in partnership with each other, continues the reign of God here on earth.

A story that makes this clear is "Becoming a Community," found in the book, *Sower's Seeds of Encouragement: Fifth Planting* (Paulist Press).

Partnership Continues God's Creation and Builds Friendship

Being a partner with someone helps to build friendships as well as continue God's work on earth. We learned the truth of this by giving students opportunities to work in pairs. For example, this is what happened in a sixth-grade class that we were teaching at St. Luke's Parish in McLean, Virginia. The Director of Religious Education at the parish had asked the class to create original expressions of the Way of the Cross that would be hung in the anteroom to the new church during Lent. We divided the class into pairs and gave each pair a large sheet of storyboard, construction paper, scissors, and glue. We talked about the Way of the Cross, then each pair chose one of the stations and began to work. The pairs worked happily and were highly imaginative in their expressions.

At the beginning of a succeeding class, in which they were to complete the stations, two of the girls who had been partners asked if they might work together again. They indicated that they hadn't known each other before and were becoming friends. When Carl and I heard this we were both happy and sad: happy because the experience had created a friendship; sad because it was February, these girls had been in the same class since October, and this had been their first opportunity to mingle and get to know each other.

Kindness is at the heart of community. It is something that everyone needs. It is something that can change the direction of a person's life and add immeasurably to the lives of many others. The power of kindness is revealed in the story, "Remember Those Who Help," in *Sower's Seeds of Encouragement: Fifth Planting* (Paulist Press).

Community Creates an Environment
Community is a primary goal in everything that we do in our religion classes and catechetical settings because it creates an environment for relationships to grow. It also provides children and young people with the experience of building friendships and maintaining them.

Within a loving community, children can learn how to listen well and experience the joy of being listened to. They can experience the self-esteem that comes from the divine being recognized and affirmed in them as well as from their own recognition and affirmation of the divine in others. They can learn how comforting it is to be helped by others, and of the need to be willing to reach out to others. Within a community of faith, children and young people can learn that they are not only witnesses of Jesus, but that they are the presence of Jesus in the world.

Children's literature is one of our greatest resources for helping children and young people capture the meaning and experience of community. The following are some of the best books that we know of on the topic, along with suggested age levels and a brief description of why and how these books might fit into a religion lesson.

The Glassmakers of Gurven, by Marlys Boddy, is a story about a small town of builders who are building themselves a church. A crisis occurs when the glassmakers can't agree on the color of glass that should go in the big window. How the glassmakers resolve their disagreement creates a delightful and wonderful story of community. This is a good book to use with third graders, especially if they are learning what it means to be "church."

Little Blue and Little Yellow, by Leo Lionni, is about two spots who are best friends. Their friendship unites them in a surprising and mysterious way. When children hear and see this story, they can grow in an understanding of what happens when they are united with Jesus in the Eucharist. We recommend this story for parents and catechists of children who are preparing for First Communion. It can also be used with fifth graders when and if they are learning more about the sacrament of Eucharist. With older children, it is possible to create imaginative versions of this story that highlight other instances of communion.

Swimmy, also by Leo Lionni, is another powerful story of community. (Both of the Lionni books are available in paperback.) We have suggested to parents that both books, especially *Little Blue and Little Yellow*, are good stories to give to their children as Christmas gifts during the year that they are preparing for First Eucharist.

Yo! Yes? by Chris Raschka, is a picture book suitable for both younger and older readers. The story is told in thirty-four words with companion illustrations that highlight the discovery of friendship, as well as the joys and insecurities that go along with reaching out to others. It is about an African-American boy who calls, "Yo!" to a shy and friendless Caucasian boy and offers him friendship. Their acceptance of each other is celebrated with a high five and the single word, "Yow." This story can be used in any lesson in which there is reflection and sharing on the theme of friendship. It is a story to read aloud while inviting listeners to read along and to act out the universal drama of choosing friendship over isolation, as well as of crossing boundaries.

One Way to Use Story in Class

Most often we use a story during the first step of a lesson. In our textbook program, *This Is Our Faith* (Silver, Burdett & Ginn), this step is called "Learning About Our Lives." As an example, the first step in Lesson One of the book for grade two contains a poem describing an experience of community. To add to the children's sense of how important community can be and is, we might also read Leo Lionni's *Swimmy* with them. We simply read it, pause, and go on to the next step in the lesson. Or, we wait for the children to make observations or ask questions about the story. We rarely raise questions about a story nor do we ever tell the children what a story means. We believe that each child receives a story in a unique and personal way. A good story rarely needs to be explained.

We have found, also, that stories take up residence in children's memories. When they are asked what they remember from previous lessons, they often will name and retell a story while seemingly not being able to recall anything else.

For Your Reflection & Response

• Think about some of the experiences of community that you enjoy. Recall some community experiences that have been part of your religion classes or that have occurred in catechetical settings.

• Try to work an aspect of community building into your next catechist in-service meeting. With each other, plan ways to help create community in the lives of your students. You might also plan an activity or two that increases community within your faculty. You might also choose stories that you'll use in one or more of your upcoming classes.

3

Seeing Others as Equal & Worthwhile

When our goddaughter Angela was considering a private Catholic high school following her eighth-grade graduation (mostly because her parents and godparents wanted her to), she applied to a prestigious Catholic girl's academy in Washington, D.C. As part of the application process, she spent a day at the school. One of the students was assigned to her as a big sister for the day. Angela was impressed with the young woman, thought she was really cool, and was pretty sure if she were accepted they might become friends—until the Sunday following the visit.

Both Angela and the young woman were at the same Mass at Holy Trinity Church. After Mass, Angela went over to the girl to say hello and talk with her. Later, Angela, told us what had happened. She said that when she approached her, the girl acted as though she didn't know her. She did not respond to Angela at all, and walked away.

Angela was really hurt and wondered aloud if she would also become a snob were she to go to that school. In the end she wasn't accepted, which was fine with her. The experience of being ignored by a potential schoolmate that she felt should have been "more Catholic" (her words) added to her lack of enthusiasm for the school. Fortunately it's an isolated incident, yet a very real one.

There is an expectancy, and rightfully so, that we who are Catholic Christians treat one another with respect, that nothing—race, color, class, creed, sex and sexual orientation, disability, clothes, education, poverty, or wealth—should make a difference. Children capture the truth of that expectancy when they are exposed to stories in which people genuinely and actively care about others no matter what they look like, no matter what their circumstances. A good example is "The Beggar King," (anonymous), found in *More Sower's Seeds: Second Planting*, by Brian Cavanaugh.

Once there was a time, according to legend, when Ireland was ruled by a king who had no son. The king sent out his couriers to post notices in all the towns of his realm. The notices advised that every qualified young man should apply for an interview with the king as a possible successor to the throne. However, all such candidates must have these two qualifications: They must first, love God and second, love their fellow human beings.

The young man around whom this legend centers saw a notice and reflected that he loved God and, also, his neighbors. One thing stopped him, he was so poor that he had no clothes that would be presentable in the sight of the king. Nor did he have the funds to buy provisions for the long journey to the castle. So the young man begged here, and borrowed there, finally managing to scrounge enough money for the appropriate clothes and the necessary supplies.

Properly attired and well-suited, the young man set out on his quest, and had almost completed the journey when he came upon a poor beggar by the side of the road. The beggar sat trembling, clad only in tattered rags. His extended arms pleaded for help. His weak voice croaked, "I'm hungry and cold. Please help me...please?"

The young man was so moved by this beggar's need that he immediately stripped off his new clothes and put on the tattered threads of the beggar. Without a second thought he gave the beggar all his provisions as well. Then, somewhat hesitantly, he continued his journey to the castle dressed in the rags of the beggar, lacking provisions for his return trek home.

Upon his arrival at the castle, a king's attendant showed him in to the great hall. After a brief respite to clean off the journey's grime, he was finally admitted to the throne room of the king. The young man bowed low before his majesty. When he raised his eyes, he gaped in astonishment. "You...it's you! You're the beggar by the side of the road."

"Yes," the king replied with a twinkle, "I was that beggar."

"But...but...but...you are not really a beggar. You are the king for real. Well, then, why did you do this to me?" the young man stammered after gaining more of his composure.

"Because I had to find out if you genuinely love God and your fellow human beings," said the king. "I knew that if I came to you as king, you would have been impressed by my gem-encrusted golden crown and my royal robes. You would have done anything I asked of you because of my regal character. But that way I would never have known what is truly in your heart.

"So I used a ruse. I came to you as a beggar with no claims on you except for the love in your heart. And I discovered that you sincerely do love God and your fellow human beings. You will be my successor," promised the king. "You will inherit my kingdom."

Another story that children find fascinating and wondrous is one that reveals two different ways of seeing. We have used this story with a photo of the famous statue "David," that Carl took in Florence. It is called "Work with Flaws," (anonymous), in *More Sower's Seeds: Second Planting*.

There is a story about two men, both Italian sculptors and contemporaries, named Donatello and Michelangelo. One day Donatello received delivery of a huge block of marble. After examining it carefully, Donatello rejected the marble because it was too flawed and cracked for him to use.

Now this was long before forklifts and hydraulic lifts, so the workmen moved the heavy load by using a series of log rollers. Rather than struggle back to the quarry, the quick-thinking haulers decided to deliver it down the street to Michelangelo. After all, he was known to be a little absent-minded. He might not realize that he had not ordered a three-ton block of marble.

When Michelangelo inspected the marble, he saw the same cracks and flaws, as did Donatello. But he also saw the block as a challenge he could not pass up. So Michelangelo accepted the block of marble that Donatello had already rejected as too flawed and too cracked to be of any use.

Michelangelo proceeded to carve from that seemingly useless block of marble what is considered to be one of the world's greatest art treasures—the statue "David."

Racism

Racism is one of the greatest evils in our society and is a pernicious affront to the truth that everyone is worthy of respect, that everyone is equally worthwhile.

Janaan's first experience with racism occurred in 1959 while she was teaching in a Catholic school on the south side of Chicago. She had forty-five children in fourth and fifth grades, all black. In October a well-known museum in the city was having a book fair. Because she wanted to increase their interest in reading she decided to take the children on a field trip to the museum. With the help of parents (chaperones), they boarded a bus and went to the museum.

All went very well until they arrived in the area of the museum where the book fair was being held. Immediately, upon seeing the color of her children, everyone on the staff in the book fair area became alert. Everywhere they went—the theater, the exhibits—an "overseer" went with them. At the same time, another group, all white children, were roaming through the book fair freely and in several instances, carelessly. None of the staff felt any need to monitor or oversee them. Janaan's children and their parents took it in stride, but she was ashamed and sickened by the experience.

About the same time Carl spent two summers with three different Native American tribes on two different Indian reservations. He was shocked at the incredible poverty and unemployment. Carl worked in the fields harvesting hay with intelligent, hard-working Indians who had left the reservations seeking good jobs and a better life in cities like Chicago, New York, and Boston. But the prejudice against them was so intense and demeaning that they came back to their reservations to find some sense of pride and self-esteem. With few jobs there, many turned to alcohol, and not a few, to suicide.

It would be a blessing if we could say that racism is a thing of the past—that in 1959 and 1960 it could be expected, but not today. Sadly, this is not so. Therefore, it is imperative that we help children see the evil of racism and refuse to be racist.

Children are not born racist. They are educated to it, sometimes very early and sometimes by members of our own families. For example, when Janaan's nephew, Brett, was in preschool, he made a friend whom he wanted to see outside of the classroom setting. One evening when his mother was putting him to bed, he asked her if his friend could come over to play. Without skipping a beat his mom asked Brett, "Isn't he black?" Brett paused for a few moments and said, "Mommy, I don't know what color he is." Fortunately, Janaan's sister realized that she was inflicting damage on his innocence and goodness, and quickly assured him that his friend was welcome to come over.

Story is a great resource for helping children to see the horror of racism and to appreciate behavior that is color-blind. A wonderful story about the power of generous, accepting behavior is "A Simple Gesture," (anonymous), in *Fresh Packet of Sower's Seeds: Third Planting*, by Brian Cavanaugh.

> History was made in the baseball world in 1947. It was in that year that Jackie Robinson became the first black player in the major leagues. The Brooklyn Dodgers' owner, Branch Rickey, told Robinson, "It'll be tough on you. You are going to take a lot of abuse, be ridiculed, and receive more verbal punishment than you ever thought possible." Rickey continued, "But I'm willing to back you all the way if you have the determination to make it work."
>
> In short order, Robinson experienced Rickey's gloomy prediction. He was abused verbally and physically as players intentionally ran him over and ran him down. The crowd was quick with racial slurs and deriding comments. Opponents, as well as his own teammates, ridiculed Robinson.
>
> Around mid-season, Robinson was having a particularly horrendous day. He had fumbled several grounders, overthrown first base, and batted poorly. The crowd that day was especially nasty. Then something miraculous happened. In front of this critical crowd, Pee Wee Reese, the team captain, walked over from his shortstop position and put his arm around Jackie Robinson.
>
> Robinson later reflected, "That simple gesture saved my career. Pee Wee made me feel as if I belonged."

The need to be color-blind is reflected in poetry as well as story. An example of this is a poem that we've often used with children called "No Difference," from *Where the Sidewalk Ends*, by Shel Silverstein.

Children's Literature and Prejudice

There are many other stories and poems about prejudice and the damage it inflicts as well as about heroism in dealing with prejudice. Here are a few examples.

Amazing Grace, by Mary Hoffman. Schoolmates tell Grace that because she's a girl and black she can't be Peter Pan in an upcoming play. But after her mother and grandmother lovingly reaffirm all possibilities, Grace tries out and plays the role to universal acclaim.

The Story of Ruby Bridges, by Robert Coles. A child braves hatred and prejudice prayerfully and courageously.

Be Good to Eddie Lee, by Virginia Fleming. Two children don't want to include another child who is disabled, but finally accept him and learn an important lesson.

Mrs. Katz and Tush, by Patricia Polacco. This is a warm and loving story of an unusual friendship between an African-American boy and an elderly Jewish neighbor.

The Witch of Blackbeard Pond, by Elizabeth George Speare. Kit, a young and lonely woman, becomes friends with a lone and mysterious figure who is known as the Witch of Blackbeard Pond. With her she feels free and at peace. But when their friendship is discovered, Kit is faced with suspicion, fear, anger, and a witch trial. This story won the John Newbery Medal.

People, by Peter Spier. This is a wonderful book that helps children appreciate people of different racial, socioeconomic, and cultural backgrounds.

The Cay, by Theodore Taylor. Philip has

looked down on black-skinned people all his life. Suddenly, he's a refugee from a fatal shipwreck, and dependent on an extraordinary West Indian man named Timothy. The two of them are cast up on a barren Caribbean Island; meanwhile, a crack on his head has left Philip blind. The story connects us with their struggle for survival, as well as with the boy's efforts to adjust to blindness and to understand the dignified, wise, and loving man who is his companion.

Let the Celebrations Begin, by Margaret Wild and Julie Vivas. In Belsen, a camp in which many Jewish people died during the Holocaust, Miriam and the Polish women plan a very special party for the children. They make incredible toys out of scraps of material, rags, torn pockets, buttons—anything. They cut and sew every night while the guards sleep. Finally, as World War II ends and the soldiers arrive to free them, the great celebration, which they planned and worked for, begins.

What about our own prejudices? Besides reading stories and poetry to children it is good to examine our own prejudices. Do we always behave as though everyone is deserving of respect, that everyone is equal and worthwhile? Perhaps what all of us need is a pair of granny's glasses, as described in the story, "Granny's Glasses," by Walter Buchanan, from *Sower's Seeds Aplenty: Fourth Planting*, by Brian Cavanaugh.

A little boy said to his playmate, "When I get older, I want to wear glasses like Granny's because she can see so much more than most people. She can see the good in a person when everyone else sees a bad side. She can see what a person meant to do even if he or she didn't do it. I asked her one day how she could see the good, and she said, it was the way she learned to look at things as she got older. And when I get older, I want a pair of glasses just like Granny's so I can see the good, too."

How different our world would be if we all wore a pair of Granny's glasses! If I would look for the good in you, and you would look for the good in me, our lives would be so much more pleasant. At times, we are like the buzzard that seeks out what is rotten and ugly, when we should be like the hummingbird that looks for what is sweet and beautiful.

I dare you to try on a pair of Granny's glasses.

For Your Reflection & Response

• There are other issues that are part of the story of equality and inequality, and many of us are affected by these issues. For example, *USA Today* (April 14-16, 2000) reported that the median earnings of women and men twenty-five years or older who worked full-time, year-round in 1998 differed by as much as $9,968. How do you feel about this kind of inequality? What are the ways that progress has been made in this area? How can the gap between the earnings of men and the earnings of women be closed even more?

• What are your feelings about people who are homosexual and lesbian? This is not always an easy issue to reflect on, yet it is necessary to do so, especially if you are working with teenagers. A book that you might consider reading is *Two Teenagers in Twenty: Writings by Gay and Lesbian Youth*, edited by Ann Heron, or *Am I Blue? Coming Out of the Silence*, edited by Marion Dane Bauer.

Treating Others with Compassion & Justice

In an article in the December 1999 issue of *U.S. Catholic*, Megan McKenna suggests that a new millennium places us at a crossroads. She says that there are some basics that the human race has never learned (and sadly, that includes Christians), but which we must learn now. The most fundamental principle to be learned, says McKenna, is perhaps best expressed in the Buddhist saying: "Do no harm." Within that saying is a call to compassion and justice, a call to respect, service, and nonviolence.

Our world is in great need of the qualities that are contained in the principle "Do no harm." Thus, compassion and justice must be fostered, modeled, inspired, taught, and expected of everyone. Children can indeed learn how to be compassionate and just; we can teach them what it looks and feels like. Our godchildren's father repeatedly tells Angela and Miguel: "We have no right to hurt anyone."

Models of compassion show up in unlikely places. Take, for example, actor Martin Sheen. In the December 7, 1999 issue of the *Washington Post* he was featured in a section called "The Reliable Source." The article indicated that he has been arrested sixty times during protests and was planning to ring in the new millennium making trouble at a Nevada nuclear testing site. "I'm thinking maybe I'll start the year in jail," he said, urging readers to join him. In the 1970s he aligned himself with Mitch Snyder in Washington, DC, during creative nonviolence protests for the homeless.

Another amazing model of compassion is John Breen of Bloomington, Indiana. He is a forty-two-year-old father of two who left a good paying job as a software programmer to do something good for the needy. With his computer skills and $20,000 of his own money he created the Hunger Site (www.thehungersite.com), a web site devoted to collecting donations to feed hungry children.

Visitors to the site don't have to buy or pay for anything in order to donate food to the poor. By simply clicking on the site's "donate free food" button once a day, people can each day see that a serving of rice, wheat, or corn goes to a hungry child somewhere in the world, at no expense to themselves. The food is paid for by companies in exchange for advertisements on the site. Each sponsor pays half a cent for each "donation," which buys a quarter cup of food. As the sponsors increase, the amount of food increases. In the middle of December, 1999, each click bought two-and-three-quarters cups of food.

Since the Hunger Site was launched in June of 1999, more than 350,000 people have clicked each day, donating a daily average of 1 million cups of food to 1 million hungry children. Michelle Singletary, a columnist who wrote about him in the *Washington Post* (December 26, 1999), asked him how he could give up his job to take on such a huge project. "I just saw that it could be done," he simply said.

In different ways, Martin Sheen and John Breen exemplify the kind of compassion Jesus speaks of in his well-known parable of the Good Samaritan (Luke 10:29–37):

> A man fell victim to robbers as he went down from Jerusalem to Jericho. They stripped and beat him and went off leaving him half-dead.
>
> A priest happened to be going down that road, but when he saw him, he passed by on the opposite side. Likewise, a Levite came to the place, and when he saw him, he passed by on the opposite side.
>
> But a Samaritan traveler who came upon him was moved with compassion at the sight. He approached the victim, poured oil and wine over his wounds and bandaged them. Then he lifted him up on his own animal, took him to an inn, and cared for him.
>
> The next day he took out two silver coins and gave them to the innkeeper with the instruction, "Take care of him. If you spend more than I have given you, I will pay you on my way back."
>
> After Jesus finished his story, he asked: "Which of these three, in your opinion, was neighbor to the robbers' victim?" A man answered, "The one who treated him with mercy. Then Jesus said to him (and to us), "Go and do likewise."

Models of Social Justice

But what if there are so many "neighbors"—poor, hungry, homeless, hurting people—that one can hardly fill all their needs? Another story can help us and those we teach discover a way to live out Jesus' call to compassion for the many who are in desperate need. Here is a true story about a man who, in his own life, discovered the face of compassion through his work for social justice. Peter J. Henriot, SJ, writes in the journal *Center Focus*:

> Dom Helder Camara, a popular, compassionate priest, was named archbishop of Recife, Brazil's poorest region. In Recife he responded quickly to ease the shocking poverty. He preached of the need for those who were blessed with more to help those who had so little. The members of his parishes responded generously.
>
> During his first years as archbishop of Recife, his people loved and admired him. As Dom Helder himself recalled, "At first the people praised me and even said that our archbishop is a saint!" But after a few years he began to ask himself and his people a challenging question. "Why is it that in such a large country, with riches of all kinds, so many people are so poor?"
>
> Reaction to Dom Helder Camara changed dramatically. His simple question, "Why?" threatened the interests of the rich and powerful. They quickly sensed the challenge of his "Why?" He was touching on the underlying causes of poverty. He was calling for structural changes in

the basic institutions of the country.

He tells us what happened then. "The people no longer called me a saint. They called me a communist and rejected me." Not long afterwards, the government banished him from Brazil. After some years they allowed him to return from exile. He became respected all over the world as a compassionate man, and a courageous model of a just man.

Dom Helder Camara's compassion for the poor led him to struggle for social justice, which for him means: "loving persons so much that I work to change the structures that violate their dignity."

More Models of Compassion and Justice
Other people who lived extraordinary lives of compassion and justice are also great models. Their stories are found in books about saints and other holy people. We recommend *Butler's Lives of the Saints*, revised by Paul Burns. The books are arranged according to the months of the year as well as to the feast-day of each saint. The life of each saint is told in detail, and when we use these books we choose the parts of a saint's life that we want to emphasize.

Other models of compassion are the young people who are service-oriented and creative in actions that make the world a better place. In an issue of the *National Catholic Reporter* (December 10, 1999) there's a report on the 1999 youth conference in St. Louis which drew 23,000 people. Keynote speaker J. Glenn Murray, SJ, told the young people gathered that, despite negative press and misconceptions about their age group, they have been "more generous and more service-oriented a generation than we have known since the 1960s."

One of the young people who addressed the session was sixteen-year-old Craig Kielburger, founder of Free the Children, an international organization working to free children from poverty and exploitation. The Toronto teen said everyone must share the gifts given by God to make the world a better place. He urged youths to live their faith through action: "When we go back to our schools, when we carry the message and we rally more people," he said, "that's how we're going to change this world."

Looking at our personal lives and those of our children is another way of learning what compassion and justice are like. Sometimes stories of missed opportunities can be very instructive.

Several years ago Janaan was going to a shopping mall with our goddaughter, Angela. She was in a hurry so she quickly passed through the doors of the entrance and had gone on a bit when she noticed Angela wasn't with her. Looking back she saw her standing outside the door seemingly with no intention to follow. Janaan hurried back to the entrance and noticed a gentleman holding out a paper cup. She had completely missed him on her way in.

But Angela had seen him. She asked Janaan, "Aren't you going to give him something?" Janaan quickly reached into her purse and pulled out a quarter. With disdain Angela looked at the quarter and asked another question, "Is that all you're going to give him?" Janaan quickly pulled a dollar out of her billfold and handed it to her. Angela turned to the man, gave him the money, chatted for a moment, and then was ready to go with Janaan into the mall.

And, still another story in which Angela was involved. We had invited Angela, her dad, and her brother to dinner. While we were discussing the time, Angela's cousin, Selena, appeared on the scene. Without hesitation, Angela asked if Selena could come, too. Janaan still can't believe that she said "No" but she did, and Angela didn't push her on it. Later that evening Janaan told Angela that not inviting Selena was unkind and thoughtless and that she was both ashamed and sorry. Angela answered, "I know, but it's all right! Selena didn't mind."

Another example of a child taking the lead in being compassionate happened on a playground of a parochial school in Chicago's Southside.

A new student had transferred to the school and for several days stood apart from clusters of other children jumping rope, playing Four Square and other games. It was Janaan's turn for playground duty, and as she watched she knew that she needed to do something to get the child included in one or other of the activities. While she was trying to figure out what to do one of the children playing Four Square walked over to the child, said something to her, and within minutes she had joined the others and was playing happily.

That incident inspired Janaan, and several years later she wrote the following poem:

> I watched you
> As you watched us
> Play.
> I saw you by yourself
> Today.
> I wonder if the gift of
> Me
> Could set the lonely in you
> Free?

Another source of instruction and inspiration are actions in families that are compassionate. For example, several years ago, while we were teaching religion to a class of sixth graders at St. Luke's in McLean, Virginia, one of our sessions was on the corporal works of mercy. Each child was asked to write and tell a story about how one of the works of mercy is exemplified in their family's life or in their own. One boy described, at length, how his mom is always going through their closets to find things to give away to the House of Ruth, Christ House, and other places that help the needy. He said, with some chagrin but with a lot of pride, that he has to hide the things he wants to keep or his mom will give them away. He added that she excuses her behavior by assuring him their family has much more than they need and that the people she gives stuff to don't have enough.

Finding Stories of Compassion and Justice in Books

Stories in books are another powerful way to learn what compassion looks and feels like. One of our favorites is "Compassion is in the Eyes," (anonymous), in *Fresh Packet of Sower's Seeds: Third Planting*, by Brian Cavanaugh.

> It was a bitter, cold evening in northern Virginia many years ago. The old man's beard was glazed by winter's frost while he waited for a ride across the river. The wait seemed endless. His body became numb and stiff from the frigid north wind.
>
> He heard the faint, steady rhythm of approaching hooves galloping along the frozen path. Anxiously, he watched as several horsemen rounded the bend. He let the first one pass by without an effort to get his attention. Then another passed by and another. Finally, the last rider neared the spot where the old man sat like a snow statue. As this one drew near, the old man caught the rider's eye and said, "Sir, would you mind giving an old man a

ride to the other side? There doesn't appear to be a passageway by foot."

Reining his horse, the rider replied, "Sure thing. Hop aboard." Seeing the old man was unable to lift his half-frozen body from the ground, the horseman dismounted and helped the old man onto the horse. The horseman took the old man not just across the river, but to his destination which was just a few miles away.

As they neared the tiny but cozy cottage, the horseman's curiosity caused him to inquire, "Sir, I notice that you let several other riders pass by without making an effort to secure a ride. Then I came up and you immediately asked me for a ride. I'm curious why, on such a bitter winter night, you would wait and ask the last rider. What if I had refused and left you there?"

The old man lowered himself slowly down from the horse, looked the rider straight in the eyes and replied, "I've been around these here parts for some time. I reckon I know people pretty good." The old timer continued, "I looked into the eyes of the other riders and immediately saw there was no concern for my situation. It would have been useless even to ask them for a ride. But when I looked into your eyes, kindness and compassion were evident. I knew, then and there, that your gentle spirit would welcome the opportunity to give me assistance in my time of need."

Those heartwarming comments touched the horseman deeply. "I'm most grateful for what you have said," he told the old man. "May I never get too busy in my own affairs that I fail to respond to the needs of others with kindness and compassion."

With that, Thomas Jefferson turned his horse around and made his way back to the White House.

Another story of compassion is "Are You Jesus?" by Brennan Manning, from *More Sower's Seeds: Second Planting*, by Brian Cavanaugh.

Several years ago a group of salesmen went to a regional sales convention in Chicago. They assured their wives that they would be home in plenty of time for Friday's supper. One thing led to another and the meeting ran overtime so the men had to race to the airport, tickets in hand. As they barged through the terminal, one man inadvertently kicked over a table supporting a basket of apples. Without stopping they all reached the plane in time and boarded it with a sigh of relief. All but one.

He paused, got in touch with his feelings, and experienced a twinge of compassion for the girl whose apple stand had been overturned. He waved goodbye to his companions and returned to the terminal. He was glad he did. The ten-year-old girl was blind.

The salesman gathered up the apples and noticed that several of them were battered and bruised. He reached into his wallet and said to the girl, "Here, please take this ten dollars for the damage we did. I hope it didn't spoil your day."

As the salesman started to walk away the bewildered girl called out to him, "Are you Jesus?" He stopped in midstride. And he wondered.

Stories of Compassion in Children's Literature

Some of the stories that we've used in religion classes with Bible stories about Jesus showing compassion are listed below.

The Bible. "The Feeding of the Five Thousand," found in Matthew 14:13–21, Mark 6:34–44, and Luke 9:10–17; "The Good Samaritan," Luke 10:29–37; "Blind Bartimaeus," Mark 10:46–52 and Luke 18:35–43.

The Book of Virtues, by William J. Bennett. "Old Mr. Rabbit's Thanksgiving Dinner," by Carolyn Sherwin Bailey; "The Legend of the Dipper," retold by J. Berg Esenwein and Marietta Stockard; "Grandmother's Table," adapted from the Brothers Grimm.

The Book of Virtues for Young People, by William J. Bennett. "If I Can Stop One Heart from Breaking," by Emily Dickinson; "The Angel of the Battlefield," by Joanna Strong and Tom. B. Leonard.

"Heaven and Hell," (anonymous); "Heroes," (anonymous), in *The Sower's Seeds*, by Brian Cavanaugh.

Stone Soup, by Marcia Brown.

The Paper Crane, by Molly Bang.

Shibumi and the Kitemaker, by Mercer Mayer.

An Angel for Solomon Singer, by Cynthia Rylant.

Tico and the Golden Wings, by Leo Lionni.

With Love at Christmas, by Mem Fox.

Saint Valentine, by Robert Sabuda.

The Story of the Jumping Mouse, by John Steptoe.

Knots On a Counting Rope, by Martin and John Archambault.

The Seeing Stick, by Jane Yolen.

An exquisite story in which the "hero" feeds the needs and hungers of the spirit and which we consider a classic compassion story is *The Dancing Man*, by Marlys Boddy. Joseph, an orphan, lives in a poor village by the Baltic Sea. He realizes, while he is still young, that life in the village is dreary and hard. No one laughs, no one dances. But he sees that all around him the world dances. He dreams that one day he will dance down the road from village to village, even as far as the southernmost sea. But he tells no one because he knows no one will understand.

Then one evening a mysterious stranger appears on the shore, sweeps off his hat, bows, and says to Joseph, "I'm the Dancing Man and I have a gift for you." The old man dances down the shore and Joseph follows. A sharp gust of wind blows Joseph around and when he turns back, the man is gone. But in the sand lay his silver shoes, and Joseph knows they are meant for him.

Joseph grows up and one day the shoes fit. He puts them on and dances from village to village, taking away some of the dreariness and bringing happiness to the people. The story ends, as it begins, with Joseph passing on to another child what had been passed on to him.

In preparing a session, determine where you feel one of the stories suggested above, or another story like these, will fit into a class. We usually read a story like this after the story from the Bible has been listened to and talked and prayed about. Frequently we invite the children to write a story or draw a picture (real or imagined) in which they have acted generously, compassionately, or unselfishly or someone has acted that way toward them.

Give your children plenty of opportunities to draw out of themselves how the principle "Do no harm" might be lived out in their daily lives.

For Your Reflection & Response

• Take some time to remember experiences and stories of compassion in your personal life, and in your life with your family, neighborhood, and parish. Look over the Sunday bulletin from your parish to discover the compassionate action that is part of your faith community. Perhaps there is an opportunity there for you to become more involved. Are there any ways that the children you are teaching might also become involved in activities that foster compassion?

• Meditate on the principle "Do no harm" and discern how this principle might govern all your relationships. Literally become a "do-gooder."

5

Making Daily Decisions through Moral Choices

In the last chapter we quoted a Buddhist principle: "Do no harm." In part, that suggests a moral stance. If we are intentional about not hurting others, we are acting like Jesus acted in his life and living out the call of our baptism—to be his disciples. In helping children to grasp what it means to do no harm and to live as disciples of Jesus, it is good to consider this question with them: "What does love look like?"

In her book *The Art of Catechesis*, Maureen Gallagher tells a brief story that in a few words describes what love looks like.

> The story is told about an atheist who went to a rabbi and said that he would become a believer if the rabbi could teach him the meaning of the whole Torah as he stood on one foot. The rabbi became enraged and threw out the atheist.
>
> The atheist went to another rabbi with the same question. The second rabbi summarized the meaning of the Torah as, "What is hateful to you, do not do to your neighbor....This is the whole Torah. All the rest is commentary."

There are other ways to describe what love looks like and one way is a change of heart, a conversion. Denise, a sixth-grader in one of our religion classes, describes this kind of conversion as she experienced it.

> I had a change of heart once when my mother and dad said my brother Eric and I should start doing more jobs around the house. My mother said she couldn't do all the small jobs in the house. I said that I didn't want to do the dishes because my new teacher gives me a lot of homework. My mother said she still shouldn't have to do all the work. Then I went to do my homework.
>
> While I was doing my homework I was thinking about what my mother said. "I

can't do all the small things plus big things!" Then I had a change of heart. I thought of my mother with her work and her larger jobs; I should do the dishes. So now I do the dishes.

Adults experience conversion, too, and this is how a teacher in one of our workshops describes her change of heart.

At the end of the school year I had the children write a letter to me, their teacher, about what they thought of class and hopefully their accomplishments. It was not an assignment, as such, that is, it was more to contain them in the few minutes before the last day's dismissal.

Later I collected the letters and took them home. The leisure I could never find heretofore I now had plenty of, and I sat down to rest and read my letters. After reading many and enjoying all, I came across one that caused me to take note and inventory.

"Dear Mrs. Slater," it began, "I loved your class and you are the best teacher I have ever had but there is one thing I'd like to tell you. When you come to the part where you ask for the homework, why do you make such a fuss when you find out I do not have mine? Don't you think you could not embarrass me by getting angry at me when you are at home? I already know when I don't have my homework—how wrong I was not to do it. I am already embarrassed.

"Now please don't stop being my friend because we are family, as you always told me, and family should be able to tell one another things on their mind."

This letter gave my ego a jolt—had I really caused this child a hurt I had no idea he had harbored? I shall collect homework in the future and no matter how much time it takes, I shall see the child after class regarding no homework—never during class. This is my conversion.

Honesty and Truthfulness

Another answer to the question "What does love look like?" is telling the truth, no matter how tempted one might be to lie. A fable that shows us what this looks like is "The Honest Woodsman," adapted from Emilie Poulsson and found in *The Children's Book of Virtues*, by William J. Bennett. It tells of a poor woodcutter who loses his axe in the river one day. As he searches the river for his axe, a water fairy appears, shows the woodsman an axe of silver, and asks if it belongs to him. The woodsman thinks for a minute of all that he could buy with the silver, but then tells the fairy that no, the silver axe was not his. The same happens as the water fairy next appears with a golden axe.

Finally, the fairy brings the lost axe up from the river bottom, and shows it to the woodsman. He says that yes, this is indeed his old axe. Then the fairy gives the woodsman his axe—along with the axes of gold and silver as a reward for his honesty.

"Honest Abe," a story in *The Children's Book of Heroes*, by William J. Bennett, is another story like the one above. Even though he had to walk three miles outside of town, Abraham Lincoln returned a mere six cents he had overcharged a customer.

Honesty and truthfulness are not easy virtues to practice. We can all recall times in our own lives when we were not as honest as we could have been. One story that Janaan told children when they have asked her if she always told the truth is one that still embarrasses her when she remembers it.

It happened at a major religious education conference. Maria Harris, a renowned speaker and professor of religious education, was giving a keynote talk. As she began she used a technique to get a sense of the historical range of her audience. She asked those who were born between 1960 and 1970 to stand. Then, in turn, she asked all who were born between 1950 and 60, then 1940 and 1950, then 1930 and 1940, then 1920 and 1930 to stand. When Maria named the years closest to Janaan's, she didn't stand even though she felt a strong pull to do so.

It may seem strange but she still feels sad about that moment. To ease the sadness we've told ourselves that it was an inconsequential lapse. As one of the eighth graders observed, however, after Janaan told the story, "It's in the small hidden things where honesty counts."

Telling the Truth after You Have Lied

After a child admitted that the hardest thing for her is to tell the truth after she's lied, Janaan wrote a poem called "My Tiger" that can be used with children to discuss that challenge:

> In my
> stomach pit
> a tiger's
> loose,
> growling,
> pawing,
> whimpering,
> racing back
> and forth.
> If I tell you
> that I lied...
> Will it help
> my tiger
> out?

Our favorite children's story about honesty is *The Empty Pot*, by Demi. Ping, a Chinese boy, loves flowers and anything he plants bursts into bloom until he and all the other children in the kingdom receive a flower seed from the Emperor with the instruction that "Whoever can show me their best in a year's time will succeed me to the throne."

Ping does everything to get his seed to bloom but it doesn't. At the end of the year he has to face the Emperor with an empty pot without a flower. He feels humiliated and sad until the reason for the seed's lack of power to grow is announced by the Emperor. Ping's honesty and integrity is revealed at that moment and he is rewarded, not only with the Emperor's great admiration, but also with being named as his successor.

Another story highlighting honesty is "Maintain Integrity," (anonymous), in *Sower's Seeds Aplenty: Fourth Planting* (Cavanaugh).

> A while back, there was a story about Reuben Gonzolas, who was in the final match of his first professional racquetball tournament. He was playing the perennial champion for his first shot at a victory on the pro circuit.
>
> At match point in the fifth and final game, Gonzolas made a super "kill shot" into the front corner to win the tournament. The referee called it good, and one of the linemen confirmed that the shot was a winner.
>
> But after a moment's hesitation, Gonzolas turned and declared that his shot had skipped into the wall, hitting the floor first. As a result, the serve went to his opponent, who went on to win the match.
>
> Reuben Gonzolas walked off the court; everyone was stunned. The next issue of a leading racquetball magazine featured Gonzolas on its cover. The lead editorial

searched and questioned for an explanation for this first-ever occurrence on the professional racquetball circuit. Who could ever imagine it in any sport or endeavor? Here was a player with everything officially in his favor, with victory in his grasp, who disqualifies himself at matchpoint and loses.

When asked why he did it, Gonzolas replied, "It was the only thing I could do to maintain my integrity."

To Love Well Is a Choice
All of us, including our children and young people, are aware that the sum total of our moral life depends upon the choices we make. Along with the question "What does love look like?" we need also to ask, "How do our actions reveal the divine operative in us?"

A story that provokes a lot of thought regarding choices as a moral legacy is "The Onion," by Fyodor Dostoevsky, in *Sower's Seeds Aplenty: Fourth Planting* (Cavanaugh).

> Once upon a time there was a peasant woman, and a very wicked woman she was. One day she died leaving not a single good deed behind. The devils caught hold of her and plunged her into the Lake of Hades.
>
> Her guardian angel stood by and wondered what good deed of hers he could remember to tell God about. The angel mentioned, "Why, she once pulled up an onion from her garden and gave it to a beggar woman."
>
> And God replied, "You take that onion then, hold it out to her in the lake, and let her take hold of it and be pulled out by it. If you can pull her out of the Lake of Hades, let her come into paradise. But if the onion breaks, then the woman must stay where she is."
>
> The angel ran to the woman and held out the onion toward her. "Come and catch hold," cried the angel. "I'll pull you out." And he began cautiously pulling her out. He had almost pulled her out when the other sinners in the lake, seeing how she was being saved, began clutching hold of her so they, too, could be pulled out.
>
> However, she was a very wicked woman and began kicking at them. "I'm to be pulled out, not you. It's my onion, not yours. Let go." As soon as she uttered these words, the onion broke. The woman fell back into the Lake of Hades where she remains to this day.
>
> And the guardian angel wept as he went away.

Stories in Children's Literature
There are many stories in children's literature that show both responding and failing to respond to the call to do the loving thing. Some of them are:

The Mightiest Heart, by Lynn Cullen. This is a compelling tale about a relationship of love between a boy and a dog. However, things happen that change the relationship, especially for the boy. In turn, this changes what the dog can do for the boy, now a man, but it does not change his love or his loyalty.

The Braids Girl, by Lisa McCourt. This is a special story of Izzy, a girl who goes, with her grandfather, to a home called the "Family Togetherness Home." Another girl is living at the home with her mother. Izzy tries to help the girl by giving her things but gradually learns that "things" are not what she needs most. With a little help from her grandfather, Izzy finally realizes that the girl longs for and needs a friend, and when Izzy offers that to the girl, everything changes.

Shoemaker Martin, by Leo Tolstoy. A shoemaker waits all day for a promised visit from Jesus. While he's waiting, he welcomes two visitors into his home and offers each of them food, drink, a warm coat, and money. He also lovingly and wisely negotiates peace and good will between a market woman and a poorly dressed boy who had stolen one of her apples. Later, when he takes his Bible down to read again the passage he has pondered all day, he learns that Jesus had visited him in the people he had helped.

The Selfish Giant, by Oscar Wilde. A once selfish giant welcomes children to his previously forbidden garden, and is eventually rewarded by an unusual tiny child.

Stories inspire. Memories of heroic actions can linger in children's imaginations and become the bedrock of their moral lives. That is a primary reason for stocking their imaginations with stories. In *The Art of Catechesis*, Maureen Gallagher suggests that stories "put flesh and blood on a religious principle and thus motivate people to respond in like manner." Here are four ways to bring story into effective play in catechetical and religious education settings.

1. Provide children with several issues of the local newspapers. Invite them to find stories that show people acting morally, that show people doing something in a loving manner.

2. Give the children many opportunities to write and tell, sketch or draw their own stories that reveal how they or someone else acted generously, honestly, lovingly, unselfishly, or responsibly—or didn't act in such a way. For example, this is what some sixth graders in one of our classes wrote on a storytelling sheet in which there were two sets of directions.

The first direction was this: "You are a follower of Jesus. He says to you, 'I came that you might have life and have it to the full' (John 10:10). Write a story of a time when someone did or said something to you that made you want to give up, that diminished how you feel about yourself."

The second direction was this: "Write another story, one that tells of a time when someone did or said something that made you do something that you thought you couldn't do, that enhanced how you feel about yourself."

Laura Campbell wrote the following story in response to the first question: "The time when someone did something that made me want to give up was when we had to do something for one of our teachers. She then started to say how terrible we were. The teacher had no faith in me or in any of the other students. It made us all feel like dirt."

Her response to the second question was this: "One day at school my teacher called me to her desk. Then she started to say that she thought I would make it in the world, that I would be able to get into a good college. This is one thing I thought I could never do."

This is what Emily Fernandez, another sixth grader, wrote in response to the first question: "The time when someone said something to me that made me feel like giving up was when my piano teacher told me that she would give me a song that I wanted, but that I wouldn't be able to play it."

And her response to the second question: "…the time when my teacher told me to do my first oral report. I was very nervous and it was hard for me to fall asleep some nights so my mother told me that everyone gets nervous the first time but then they don't get as nervous anymore. So the day I did my report I did it fine and got a A+."

3. Connect stories from children's literature,

from the newspapers, and the children's own stories with stories in the Bible that are about Jesus doing the loving thing.

4. Use poetry. One poem that we have used, especially with fifth graders, although it works with older children as well, is "A Sad Song About Greenwich Village" by Frances Park, found in *On City Streets: An Anthology of Poems*, selected by Nancy Larrick.

> She lives in a garret
>   Up a haunted stair,
> And even when she's frightened
>   There's nobody to care.
>
> She cooks so small a dinner
>   She dines on the smell,
> And even if she's hungry
>   There's nobody to tell.
>
> She sweeps her musty lodging
>   As the dawn steals near,
> And even when she's crying
>   There's nobody to hear.
>
> I haven't seen my neighbor
>   Since a long time ago,
> And even if she's dead
>   There's nobody to know.

We usually read the poem aloud twice. Then after a silent pause, we invite anyone in the class who wishes to do so, to tell how they feel about the poem's story. Further activity might involve a discussion around the answers to questions such as these: Is the woman anyone's responsibility? What could change that woman's situation? Do you know anyone who is totally alone? Are there organizations in the community or groups in the parish who help people like this woman? Have you ever participated in action for the poor?

Finally we might have the children, either individually or as part of the whole group, write a four-stanza poem in which the woman's life is different.

In this chapter we have touched on only a few stories which reveal what love looks like. It is a limited attempt to give you some ideas on how to use story to teach morality.

For Your Reflection & Response

- Think about how the Buddhist principle "Do no harm" is operative in your life.

- Choose to read a book and/or see a movie that deals with a moral issue or question.

- With the faculty, consider moral issues that are part of your parish or school situation. Plan ways to deal with these situations in an effective way. Also, you might plan how to affirm the good that is evident and continually going on in your faith community.

Beginning Anew through Forgiveness & Reconciliation

God is present and active in our efforts to forgive and to reconcile. When we forgive and reconcile, we're responding to the promptings of God's grace and mercy. The divine in us is operative. Helping children to recognize the value of forgiving and reconciling, as well as to inspire them to be forgiving and reconciling, is at the heart of what we do as catechists and religion teachers.

Yet teaching the art of forgiveness and reconciliation is hard. Experiences of reconciliation and forgiveness happen in relationships, primarily between two parties, and the causes of the rift or breakdown are often completely or partially hidden. Nevertheless, it is vital to overcome the hardships because a community's life and spirit suffer when some of its members cannot or will not forgive and reconcile. A story that mirrors that truth is "The Clump of Grass," by Brian Cavanaugh, in his book *Fresh Packet of Sower's Seeds*.

A story is told about a village on a South Pacific Island where a missionary made his monthly visit to celebrate the Mass, baptize children and new initiates, witness marriage vows, anoint the sick, and pray for the recently deceased.

In this particular village a unique custom is practiced whenever the missionary arrives in his seaplane. By tradition, the village chief is the first to greet the padre when he steps on the land. The two of them embrace, then the chieftain gives the priest a clump of dune grass. The priest returns the clump of grass to the chief, who then turns and gives it to the person next to him. According to island custom, the clump of earth and grass is a sacred reminder of God's presence to the people who live with the vast ocean about them. The islanders consider it a type of sacramental symbolizing harmony and peace.

The sacred clump of grass passes from

one villager to the next, throughout the entire village, until it returns to the chief, who then presents it to the priest, completing the ritual. The custom with the sacred clump of grass symbolizes that the villagers are in harmony with one another and are at peace. It is at this point that the Mass can begin, and not before.

On this particular visit the padre went about his other duties as usual. When the customary time neared for the joyous celebration of the Eucharist, word came to the priest that there was going to be a delay. It seems that there was a bitter disagreement between a father and son, and the clump of grass had not been exchanged between them. There was no celebration of the Mass that month or the next. It took three months before harmony and peace were restored to that family and to the island village.

Forgiveness and Reconciliation Can Happen Ritually in a Community

Hardly a day goes by without reasons for expressing reconciling statements like, "I'm sorry, please forgive me," "It's okay, I know you didn't mean it," "I forgive you," "Let's just forget the whole thing and move on."

It's healthy and healing when hurts and wrongs are dealt with when they happen. A wonderful story about this way of forgiving and reconciling is revealed in the story, "Tribal Ritual for Antisocial Behavior," in *Sower's Seeds of Encouragement: Fifth Planting* (Paulist Press).

Sometimes forgiveness and reconciliation just don't happen. The worst possible scenario is when days, months, and years go by and forgiving and reconciling don't take place. An example of this is found in a story called "The Berry Spoon," by an anonymous author, in *Sower's Seeds Aplenty* (Cavanaugh).

"I'll never forgive him. I told him I would never forgive him."

The elderly lady spoke softly, but with resolve, as the nurse brought her her nightly medication. The lady's expression was troubled as she turned away, focusing on the drape wrapped around her nursing home bed. This brief exchange revealed a deep, deep hurt.

She told of how her brother had approached her bed, accusing her of taking more than her share of family heirlooms following their mother's death. He spoke of various items, ending with "the berry spoon." He said, "I want the berry spoon." For the forty years since the mother's death he had hidden his feelings, and now they erupted.

She was both hurt and angered by his accusation and vowed never to forgive him. "It's my spoon. Mother gave it to me," she defended herself. "He's wrong and I won't forgive him."

Standing at her bedside, the nurse felt her own spirit soften and grieve. A spoon—a berry spoon! In the bed lay a woman given two months to live—just sixty days—and she would face eternity and never see her brother again in this life. Her mind and spirit were in anguish, and her only remaining family ties were broken over a berry spoon.

As the nurse returned to her station she was drawn deep into thought: "How many berry spoons are there in my life? How many things, as insignificant as a spoon, in light of eternity, separate me from God—and from others? How does a lack of forgiveness keep me separated from my family?"

She asked God to search her heart. "How many berry spoons are there in my life?"

There are also instances when forgiveness is both given and received, in spite of heartbreaking circumstances. A powerful story of that is recorded in "Forgiveness Begins New Life," by Doris Donnelly, in *Sower's Seeds Aplenty* (Cavanaugh).

One day a seven-year-old boy was riding in the back seat of the family car. He was sitting between his older brother and sister. Their mother was driving.

On this day their mother was feeling especially distraught over having been recently abandoned by their father. Suddenly, in a fit of anger, she spun around and slapped the seven year old across the face. She yelled at the boy: "And you! I never wanted you. The only reason I had you was to keep your father. But then he left anyway. I hate you."

That scene branded itself on the boy's memory. Over the years his mother reinforced her feelings toward him by constantly finding fault with him. Years later that son was able to tell his counselor, "I can't tell you how many times in the last twenty-three years I relived that experience. Probably thousands."

He continued, "But recently I put myself in my mother's shoes. Here she was, a high school graduate with no skills, no job, no money, and a family to support. I realized how lonely and depressed she must have felt."

He continued, "I thought of the anger and the pain that must have been there. And I thought of how much I reminded her of the failure of her young hopes. And so one day I decided to visit her and talk to her. I told her that I understood her feelings and that I loved her just the same.

"She broke down and we wept in each other's arms for what seemed to be hours. It was the beginning of a new life for me, for her—for both of us."

Another story of that kind of forgiveness is "Loving Your Enemies," (anonymous), in *The Sower's Seeds* (Cavanaugh).

Abraham Lincoln tried to love, and he left for all history a magnificent drama of reconciliation.

When he was campaigning for the presidency, one of his arch enemies was a man named Edwin McMasters Stanton. For some reason Stanton hated Lincoln. He used every ounce of his energy to degrade Lincoln in the eyes of the public. So deep-rooted was Stanton's hate for Lincoln that he uttered unkind words about his physical appearance, and sought to embarrass him at every point with the bitterest diatribes. But in spite of this, Lincoln was elected the sixteenth president of the United States of America.

Then came the period when Lincoln had to select his cabinet, which would consist of the persons who would be his most intimate associates in implementing his programs. He started choosing men here and there for the various positions.

The day finally came for Lincoln to select the all-important post of Secretary of War. Can you imagine whom Lincoln chose to fill this post? None other than the man named Stanton.

There was an immediate uproar in the president's inner circle when the news began to spread. Advisor after advisor was heard saying, "Mr. President, you are making a mistake. Do you know this man Stanton? Are you familiar with all the ugly things he said about you? He is your enemy. He will seek to sabotage your programs. Have you thought this through, Mr. President?"

Mr. Lincoln's answer was terse and to the point: "Yes, I know Mr. Stanton. I am aware of the terrible things he has said about me. But after looking over the nation, I find he is the best man for the job." So Stanton became Abraham Lincoln's Secretary of War and rendered an invaluable service to his nation and his president.

Not many years later Lincoln was assassinated. Many laudable things were said about him. But of all the great statements made about Abraham Lincoln, the words of Stanton remain among the greatest. Standing near the dead body of the man he once hated, Stanton referred to him as one of the greatest men who ever lived and said, "He now belongs to the ages."

If Lincoln had hated Stanton both men would have gone to their graves bitter enemies. But through the power of love Lincoln transformed an enemy into a friend. This is the power of redemptive love.

Other forgiveness, healing, and reconciliation stories in Brian Cavanaugh's collections are "Love For Others: A Hasidic Story," (anonymous), in *The Sower's Seeds*; "Christmas Cookies," by Pat Stackhouse, in *Sower's Seeds Aplenty: Fourth Planting*; and "Reconcile Petty Squabbles," (anonymous), in *Fresh Packet of Sower's Seeds: Third Planting*.

Forgiveness and Reconciliation in Children's Literature

Most of us, including our children and young people, find stories of forgiveness and reconciliation inspiring and instructive. They can be catalysts for searching out the stories of forgiveness and reconciliation that have occurred in our own lives. They can also increase our awareness of the importance of helping young people to be forgiving and reconciling. There are many stories of this type in children's literature. Here are some of the ones we recommend for use at home or in the classroom.

The Legend of the Persian Carpet, by Tomie de Paola. A precious diamond, loved by a king and his people, is stolen from the palace. When the sun had reflected through the diamond, the rooms were filled with a million rainbows of light and color. Without the diamond, they were filled with shadows and gloom. The king is devastated until a young boy finds a way to bring the colors back to the room and the king back to his people. This is a story of turning from darkness to light, healing and restoration.

Even If I Did Something Awful? by Barbara Shook Hazen. A child has broken one of her mother's treasures and to make sure of her mother's forgiveness and unconditional love, she keeps identifying different scenarios and repeating the question, "Even if I did something awful?"

A Bargain for Frances, by Russell Hoban. Frances and Thelma are friends but Frances frequently gets the bad end of a deal when she plays with Thelma. When Frances is going to Thelma's to play tea party and make mud cakes, her mother warns Frances to be careful. She doesn't want her to be hurt again. Thelma, however, being Thelma, does indeed make a bad faith bargain with Frances.

When Frances finds out she's been taken, she cleverly figures out a way to right the wrong and save the friendship. This story not only deals with breaking faith in a relationship, it also reveals how important reconciliation is to maintaining friendships.

And to Think that We Thought that We'd Never Be Friends, by Mary Ann Hoberman. This is a story of "making up" which is the activity of reconciling. Children understand the phrase "making up" because it's something they do in their families and with their friends. This story also reveals the power that "making up" has to create harmony and community. It is a fast moving, fun-filled, imaginative celebration of friendship, peace, and collaboration.

The Rag Coat, by Lauren Mills. Minna's father is dead, her family is poor, and she doesn't have a coat to wear to school when it gets cold. A group of mothers who quilt together decide to make Minna a coat out of rags, scraps of old clothing. When Minna goes to school in the rag coat the other children make fun of her coat. She is saddened by their behavior and goes to the woods and sits on a log. While there she remembers some words of her father, and cries. She then goes back to school, shares the stories of the rags in her coat, and acceptance and forgiveness occur.

The Crystal Heart: A Vietnamese Legend, by Aaron Shepard. Mi Nuong, the daughter of a great mandarin, hears a song that floats to her from a distance. She thinks it may be a mandarin's son in disguise—the man she is destined to marry. She waits and waits by her window hoping to hear the singer again. When she doesn't, she becomes ill.

To help her get well the great mandarin sends a messenger to locate the person who sang the song. The fisherman doesn't understand what is going on as he is taken to Mi Nuong's closed door to sing the song. When Mi Nuong hears the song she orders the door open. When the fisherman sees Mi Nuong he falls hopelessly, desperately in love with her. But Mi Nuong, noting that he is a common fisherman, laughs at her folly.

The fisherman is deeply hurt, grows ill, and dies. His body is found by the villagers, who notice that there is a large crystal heart on his chest. They take the crystal heart and put it in a boat to float down to the sea, but it washes ashore by the mandarin's palace where it is found by the mandarin. He picks it up and has it made into a tea cup for his daughter. When she goes to sip tea from it the face of the fisherman is on the surface of the tea and his sweet song fills the room.

Mi Nuong remembers the fisherman's eyes and her laugh. She realizes how cruel she was. Her eyes fill with tears of sorrow and one drops into the cup. The crystal melts away, releasing the spirit of the fisherman. She later marries but she still often hears the song of the fisherman echo softly in her heart.

Using These Stories in Class
One way that we have successfully used stories of forgiveness is to dramatically read or tell them. We then invite two or three volunteers to retell the story using their own words. Others in the group are given an opportunity to fill in what was left out in the retelling or indicate parts in the retelling that were not in the original.

Another interesting and meaningful activity is to put the children in pairs or small groups, then tell them to change the ending of the story and give reasons for the change. Sometimes, we also ask "What if?" questions about the story.

Yet another activity is to work together as a group to create a mural of the story. Or, give the children a chance to write or draw their own stories about experiences of forgiving or being forgiven.

Questions that you may want to ask of a story are: How do you feel about what happened in the story? What do you think you will always remember about this story? What other stories have you heard that are like this one?

Sometimes we pause after a story to give everyone an opportunity to silently think of things that we have done which we might regret, as well as of things that we need to forgive. Then, still in silence, we plan how we will forgive both ourselves and others. We might also pray the "Our Father" together, placing special emphasis on the phrase "Forgive us our trespasses as we forgive those who trespass against us."

Helping Children Forgive and Reconcile

• Be alert to signs of unkindness and hurtful behavior among and between the children in your group. Talk to them individually and together about what is going on. Invite them to come up with ways to change what is going on, to forgive, to reconcile.

• Be quick to say, "I'm sorry" if you say something to a child or to the group that is unkind, thoughtless, diminishing, or prejudicial.

• Give the children opportunities to write stories. You can ask them to "Write a story about a time when someone did or said something to you that made you feel hurt, sad, wronged"; or, "Write a story about a time when you said unkind things to or about someone else. What happened? How did you make it right?"; or "Write a story about something you did that you thought was so bad it couldn't be forgiven. What happened?"

• Be on the alert for stories in the daily newspapers that are about forgiving and reconciling, and read them with the children.

• With the children, act out scenarios of being hurt and of healing.

• Give the children opportunities to draw pictures of forgiving and of not forgiving.

• Make peace and harmony hallmarks of your class community.

• Make a banner that says, "Remember, God forgives you everything, yes, everything!" and hang it where it can be easily seen.

For Your Reflection & Response

• Remember some of your own stories of forgiveness and reconciliation. Is there someone that you should forgive or reconcile with? Is there someone from whom you need to ask forgiveness? How do you respond when someone forgives you?

• A narrative poem by John Shea, "A Prayer For The Lady Who Forgave Us," found in his book *The Hour of the Unexpected*, pinpoints believable responses: a denial of sinfulness, a distrust of forgiveness, and a disdain for the messenger. The surprise ending hints at the loss when a prophetic voice is stilled. Read it below, ponder it, enjoy it.

There is
a long suffering lady
with thin hands
who stands on the corner
of Delphia and Lawrence
and forgives you.

"You are forgiven,"
she smiles.

The neighborhood is embarrassed.
It is sure
it has done nothing wrong
yet everyday
in a small voice
it is forgiven.

On the way to the Jewel Food Store
housewives pass her
with hard looks
then whisper
in the cereal section.

Stan Dumke asked her
right out
what she was up to
and
she forgave him.

A group
who care about the neighborhood
agreed that if she was old
it would be harmless
or if she was religious
it would be understandable
but as it is...
they asked her to move on.

Like all things
with eternal purposes
she stayed.
And she
was informed
upon.

On a most unforgiving day
of snow and slush
while she was reconciling
a reluctant passerby
the State People,
whose business is sanity,
persuaded her into a car.

She is gone.
We are reduced
to forgetting.

7

God's Presence Sustains Us

Presence is an extraordinary concept in the Catholic Christian tradition. Its meaning is connected with the presence of Christ in the assembly that gathers for Mass, the priest presider, the Scripture readings, and the bread and wine. His eucharistic presence celebrates and reminds us of his presence with us at every moment through people and all creation.

The poem "Remember," by Christy Kenneally, found in his book *Miracles and Me*, describes Jesus speaking to his disciples at the Last Supper. In this poem, Jesus asks the disciples to remember the many ways he had been with them, and tells them that he will continue to be with them in the bread and wine that they share when they gather as a community to pray.

> Remember Jesus said,
> "Remember times we had,
> Times when we were happy,
> Times when we were sad,
> Times we spent together,
> In the dark and light.
> Remember our togetherness,
> Remember it tonight."

> Remember Jesus said,
> "Remember how we shared.
> When anyone had any need
> Remember how we cared.
> Remember how our friendship
> Made every burden light.
> Remember all our sharing.
> Remember it tonight."

> Remember Jesus said,
> "Remember what I do.
> I take this simple bread and wine
> And give myself to you.
> Remember in the days to come,
> Remember when you share
> This bread and wine
> As friends of mine,
> Remember, I am there."

God Is Present in All of Creation

We also believe in the presence of God in all creation which includes the human family. When we talk about God's presence, we say things like, "God is the divine in us" or "God dwells in our hearts," or we use the word "soul" to identify God's indwelling.

To awaken children to God's presence and

to continually deepen their sense of the presence of the divine in them is to transform their lives and equip them to live faithfully, lovingly, joyfully, and with hope. One way we can capture children's imagination about God's presence is to provide them with meaningful and creative answers to the question, "What is God like?" One example is found in the book *The Runaway Bunny*, by Margaret Wise Brown. This story is about a little bunny who wants to run away. His mother's response is, "If you run away I will run after you. For you are my little bunny." The bunny narrates a number of ways that will make it possible for him to get away and his mother lovingly counters each one by telling him how she will find him.

God, like the mother in the story, promises to be with us always, wherever we go. God is also like a pursuing hound as is described in Francis Thompson's great poem, "The Hound of Heaven." This poem can be found in many different books, but one we recommend is *The Loyola Book of Verse*, edited by John Quinn. In the opening stanza we see the same image as is revealed in *The Runaway Bunny*.

> I fled Him, down the nights
>   and down the days;
> I fled Him down the arches of the years;
> I fled Him down the labyrinthine ways
> Of my own mind; and in the mist of tears
> I hid from Him, and under running laughter.
>   Up vistaed hopes I sped;
>   And shot precipitated,
> Adown Titanic glooms of chasmed fears,
>   From those strong Feet that followed,
>   followed after.

Presence Comforts and Strengthens

God's presence is revealed in someone who sits in silence with another. For a period in Carl's life he regularly visited the Boys' Industrial School in Topeka, Kansas. It was a state institution set up to rehabilitate adolescent boys who were sent there by the courts for minor and major crimes.

Carl's assignment was to teach the Catholic inmates once a week. One Sunday it happened that one of his students was confined to a solitary room for some violation. Carl got permission to sit with him in that locked room for an hour. He sat down with the boy and tried to start up a conversation. The boy did not respond. So Carl sat silently with him until the hour was up. As a guard began to unlock the door for Carl, the boy looked at Carl and asked him in a tone of wonder, "Why did someone like you sit here for an hour with a bum like me?"

Several years later someone else's quiet presence was like a balm in Carl's life. While he was a student in Innsbruck, Austria, he became very ill. Far away from St. Louis and home, not completely fluent in the German language, he was not only ill but feeling alone and lonely. One afternoon a fellow student quietly entered Carl's room as he was resting, pulled a chair near to Carl's bed and simply sat with him for a good part of the afternoon. It was an unexpectedly kind gesture, one that was healing and one that helped Carl make the difficult decision to return to the United States to recuperate and pursue his studies there.

God is like someone whose presence creates a relationship that comforts and strengthens. This is exquisitely revealed in the story, "The Empty Chair Prayer" in *Sower's Seeds that Nurture Family Values: Sixth Planting* (Paulist Press).

Presence Is a Giving of Self

Another story that reveals God's gift of presence is "The King's Great Gift," (anonymous), in *Fresh Packet of Sower's Seeds*.

> There once was a wise and beloved king who cared greatly for his people and wanted only what was the best for them. The people knew the king took a personal interest in their affairs and tried to understand how his decisions affected their lives. Periodically, he would disguise himself and wander through the streets, trying to see life from their perspective.
>
> One day he disguised himself as a poor villager and went to visit the public baths. Many people were there enjoying the fellowship and relaxation. The water for the baths was heated by a furnace in the cellar, where one man was responsible for maintaining the comfort level of the water. The king made his way to the basement to visit with the man who tirelessly tended the fire.
>
> The two men shared a meal together, and the king befriended this lonely man. Day after day, week in and week out, the king went to visit the firetender. The man in the cellar soon became close to his strange visitor because he came down to the basement where he was. No one else ever had showed that much caring and concern.
>
> One day the king revealed his true identity to his friend. It was a risky move, for he feared that the man might ask him for special favors or a gift. Instead, the king's new friend looked into his eyes and said, "You left your comfortable palace to sit with me in this hot and dingy cellar. You ate my meager food and genuinely showed you cared about what happens to me. On other people you might bestow rich gifts, but to me you have given the greatest gift of all. You gave me the gift of yourself."

Wind and air, one and the same atmospheric reality, are often connected to God's mysterious presence. They help us to believe in a God that we can't see because the wind and air can't be seen either. They are vital to our existence, which is also true of God's presence in our lives and in the whole of creation.

A poem that deals with the wind's unseen presence in a near mystical way is "Who Has Seen the Wind," by Christina Rossetti.

> Who has seen the wind?
> Neither I nor you;
> But when the leaves hang trembling,
> The wind is passing through.
>
> Who has seen the wind?
> Neither you nor I;
> But when the leaves bow down their heads,
> The wind is passing by.

Another poem, "Mountain Wind," by Barbara Kunz Loots, captures the same mystery of unseen presence.

> Windrush down the timber chutes
> between the mountain's knees—
> a hiss of distant breathing,
>   a shouting in the trees,
>   a recklessness of branches,
>   a wilderness a-sway,
>   when suddenly
> a silence
> takes your breath away.

Both of these poems can be found in the *Random House Book of Poetry for Children*, selected by Jack Prelutsky.

Other Children's Literature Selections

The Collector of Moments, by Quint Buchholz. A solitary boy is befriended by Max, an artist. The boy spends days in Max's studio, and each evening at dusk he plays his violin. Sometimes the artist sings along; sometimes he's just silent. But no matter how much time the boy spends in the studio he is never allowed to see the paintings until the artist goes on a journey, leaving behind a surprise exhibition for the boy. The boy studies each of the pictures and discovers answers to all his questions.

After the boy has spent time pondering each of the paintings, the artist returns to get his things and to move on. Before he leaves, he tells the boy that he is a very special person and, by all means, he should continue to make music.

The boy misses his friend, until one day a box arrives from the artist with a new picture and a message. He tells the boy that his music is always there in his pictures. This gives the boy a sense of his continued connection with the artist and helps him accept his own gift, which he eventually uses to inspire and teach others.

Shalinar's Song, by Daniel J. Porter. Shalinar is the son of the Master Builder of the Kingdom. When Shalinar is six he surprises his father with the song his hammer makes as it hits the chisel on its mark. His father tells him, "The song of God is in your heart, Shalinar. It rings through the work you do. Always think of God as you work and your labor will shine."

Shalinar grows up, and after his father dies he becomes the Master Builder of the Kingdom. He surpasses his father's skill in the buildings he creates but he fails or refuses to listen to the song of God in his heart. When he is old and living in a magnificent mansion that he built for himself, he feels lonely and empty until one day when he hears beautiful music from a flute that is played by a small boy.

The time he spends listening to the boy playing his flute eventually brings Shalinar back to his father's words, "The song of God is in your heart, Shalinar." After a false start, Shalinar recovers the song of God in his heart and mysteriously, to this day, continues to sing it in the kingdom where he was once Master Builder.

In God's Name, by Sandy Eisenberg Sasso. All the people of the world set out to find God's name. Each one, in turn, names God according to what he or she feels and believes God is like, for example: Source of Life, Creator of Light, Shepherd, Maker of Peace, My Rock, Healer, Redeemer, Ancient One, Comforter, Mother, Father, Friend. They all believe their name for God is the right one until each person who has a name for God looks at the others who have different names. Then they look into a lake that is clear and quiet like a mirror, God's mirror, and see their own faces and the faces of all the others. In so doing they realize that all the names for God are good and no name is better than another. In the end their voices come together and they call God One.

God's Presence Is Revealed in Our Behavior

The most convincing stories of God's presence are told in the ways we are present to children and young people. This was made very clear to us one year while Janaan was teaching sixth grade.

For lack of a classroom, they were working together around a table in an office in the Religious Education Center. One of the boys, as soon as he got bored—which was often—would slip under the table and take up residence there. Every time he did this it entertained the other children in the class and tended to throw Janaan off balance. She would then spend a miserable few moments getting him to rejoin the group above the table.

One day, however, feeling more than usually frustrated, Janaan too slipped under the table and simply looked into the boy's eyes. Not sure how to handle her being under the table with him, he slowly backed up and took his place above the table. Still feeling a bit unsure Janaan stayed a few moments longer under the table, enjoying the awful quiet that had descended on the group. When she was ready she too took her place above the table and continued the class as though nothing untoward had happened.

The boy never slipped under the table again, although he was creative in doing other things to keep Janaan off balance. But no matter what he did, she did not give up on him. She kept thinking, "there's gold in dem dar hills."

Janaan's positive approach toward that boy really paid off. One afternoon, three months later, he was helping Janaan put the room back in order. The other children had gone and they were working in silence, hurrying to get the job done. Suddenly, the boy spoke and said, "Ms. Manternach, you're different!" Her first response was a silent "ouch." But then he went on: "You think I'm all right!" We will never forget that moment because it taught us that our behavior affects kids more than anyone can imagine.

Another story is about a teacher who worked with us in teaching a fifth-grade class. She would take over teaching the class when we were traveling to do workshops. One Sunday our out-of-town workshop had been canceled so we decided to go to the class as participants, not catechists. After the session, we were walking down the corridor, talking with several of the kids, when one of them remarked with great appreciation, "You know whenever I see Miss Claudia, I think of God."

Our loving and caring presence in children's lives can help them to believe in the presence of a loving and caring God, someone who is always with them and for them, someone who will never abandon them, someone who will pursue them like Thompson's "Hound of Heaven" or like the mother in *The Runaway Bunny*.

For Your Reflection & Response

• Spend some time reflecting on God's presence in your life. How does it make a difference in the way you are?

• Read the poem below, "End of the Beginning," by Jim Northrup, from the collection, *Pierced by a Ray of Sun*, selected by Ruth Gordon, and chew on the last two lines.

Someone said we begin to die
the minute we're born.
Death is a part of life.
Who knows why the Creator
thins the herd.

Another old saying says
we must all be prepared
to give up those we love
or die first.
Take time to mourn.
Take time to remember.
Everything happens in cycles.
The pain you feel was once
balanced by someone's joy
when that baby was born.
The loss you feel today
will be replaced by good
long-lasting memories.

Is there a message here? Yeah,
treat others like this
is your last day above ground.

Living the Sabbath with Rest & Presence

The Jubilee year 2000 re-introduced the word and meaning of "Sabbath" into our religious vocabulary and consciousness.

In her book *Proclaim Jubilee*, Maria Harris writes that in the Old Testament, all farmland was to lie fallow for the duration of the Jubilee year. In other words, no crops other than those that were necessary were to be planted so that the earth could rest. She then tells us that today we can honor our relationship with the earth by attending to a different land, that is, the land of ourselves. And so during a Jubilee year, we are to let this land lie fallow, the land of our bodies, our blood, our breath, and our bones. Like celebrating Sabbath, Jubilee is a time when we should refrain from doing anything that takes us away from God.

Why does the word "Sabbath" seem new? Admittedly, we ourselves have not done much at all in teaching children about Sabbath during our years of writing religious education materials, working with religion teachers and catechists, and in catechetical sessions with children. Nor has much attention been given to this topic by others, whether in homilies at Mass and or in adult education. It is important to change that situation, and to instruct both ourselves and our children about honoring Sabbath. We must all make Sabbath a part of our lives.

A Wake-up Call

Once in awhile we are all given a wake-up call with regard to the need to let the tiny country of our body rest. Several years ago Janaan got one of those wake-up calls.

We had just finished a summer-long stint of fifteen workshops throughout the United States and were into our fall commitments, one of which was a diocesan religious education conference in Illinois. The night before we were scheduled to leave, Janaan got very little sleep because of an onset of diarrhea. By the next morning she was feeling a bit better but decided to rest until our flight that afternoon.

When we left for the airport Janaan wasn't feeling well—but she wasn't feeling bad either. While we were waiting in the departure lounge, however, the diarrhea recurred and she began to feel weak and feverish. Carl made an on-the-spot decision to cancel our trip, managed to get our luggage back off the plane, and called the diocesan office from the airport to cancel. We then took a cab home.

Shortly after we got home Janaan went to the emergency room with a temperature of 104 degrees, a high white blood cell count, dehydration, and vomiting. For three days none of the antibiotics the doctors gave her could relieve the fever. Because of the assault on her body, she went into congestive heart failure—"code blue"—and just about didn't make it.

Fortunately Janaan pulled through, but the morning before she left the hospital the head nurse came in, sat down, and talked to her about taking care of her body. She asked her questions about her lifestyle and told her that had she gotten on the plane to Illinois, she would not have survived. The nurse then urged Janaan to spend at least fifteen minutes every day getting in touch with what was going on in her life, to reflect on how she was treating her body, to discern the outside pressures that were controlling her life, and to figure out how to deal with those pressures. She ended by telling Janaan, "Other people have plans for you, you have plans for you, and your body has plans—and your body will win."

Very sobered by what had occurred we made some changes in our lives. One major one was that, except for unusual circumstances, we would only do one out-of-town talk a month.

There are a number of signs that signify a need for Sabbath in our lives. Depression, burn-out, crankiness, not being able to sleep well, chronic illnesses, and restlessness can be signals that the land of ourselves needs time to lie fallow. Some of these signs can also be present in children and young people, who also need Sabbath.

If we're going to help ourselves and our children honor Sabbath we need to know what it means to live by Sabbath and as Sabbath. Sabbath means we consciously live in the present. We all dwell in time, and we don't necessarily think about time all that much, except to exclaim about how fast it goes.

Janaan's mom, who is ninety-six, frequently complains about the rapid passage of time. She is often distressed that she doesn't have enough time to do all the things she has to do and wants to do. Unfortunately, most of us feel that way. When and how, then, can we fit Sabbath practice into the time that we and our children have?

A Weekly Sabbath
One place to start is the weekly twenty-four-hour period most essential to Sabbath practice and most honored as its centerpiece. This Sabbath begins weekly at midnight every Saturday and ends at midnight every Sunday.

Janaan first experienced this concept of Sabbath as a child growing up on a farm near Cascade, Iowa. Like most of the other families in that area, her family kept the Sabbath holy. This was a commandment that was adhered to strictly, its roots found in Exodus 20:8–10: "Remember the sabbath day, and keep it holy. Six days you shall labor and do all your work. But the seventh day is a sabbath to the Lord your God; You shall not do any work."

On the farm, Sabbath day began with only the chores that were necessary. The rest of the day was literally one of rest. If and whenever it was necessary to work in the fields on Sunday, Janaan recalls that her dad would ask permission to do so from their parish priest. She also remembers being worried about one of the neighbors, also Catholic, who was considered to be living in serious sin because he regularly worked on Sunday.

We were recently reminded of this strict way of keeping Sabbath while visiting our goddaughter, Angela, a student at the University of Valencia in Spain. She lives with a host family who, like her, is Catholic. The two Sundays we were there, Angela wondered aloud about her host family. "Can you believe this? They go to Mass, have a nice meal, and do nothing but go for walks or a movie, play games, sleep. That's all they ever do on Sunday. They simply push the pause button on life. It's hard for me to even think about doing nothing for a whole day—actually I usually get most of my homework done on Sunday."

That is what Angela has learned from the significant adults in her life because none of us keep Sabbath, except for regularly going to Mass. During her whole twenty years we have all been as busy on Sunday as we are on any other day of the week—doing some different things, yes, but working like every other day. (Actually, Angela knows that Sunday is one of Janaan's best writing days.)

Daily Sabbaths

Angela has learned a lot about Sabbath from her sojourn in Spain. Another thing that is practiced there is a daily Sabbath. Nearly everything closes down from 3:00 PM to 5:00 or 5:30 PM. Stores are closed, banks are closed, the Cathedral is closed, museums are closed. Some restaurants remain open because, along with a siesta, the main meal is eaten during this time, but many of them are also closed.

It is true that here in the United States we take time off for lunch, but many times, we eat at our desks or on the run. Some employees, most notably college professors and those in religious life, do have six-month- to year-long sabbaticals but even during those times a research or writing project is usually in the works. Our American spirit and soul are simply not geared to spending time in non-productive activities, including rest. We are not adept at "non-doing," although many of us yearn to be. In our home, we have a poster that we like—even though its wisdom is not operative in our lives. The picture on the poster shows a large animal resting peacefully near the words, "I love to do nothing and then rest afterwards."

Many people, however, including Carl, believe enough in daily Sabbath to take five- to ten-minute pauses before they start work. One woman we know from our parish takes a daily, ten-minute Sabbath at her computer, guided by a Web site named Sacred Space (www.jesuit.ie/prayer). She claims that her whole body is calmed and refreshed during this time and that this practice makes a great difference in her way of being during the rest of the day.

There are other kinds of daily Sabbaths. Several years ago we attended a session on prayer and were genuinely inspired by the woman who gave it. She is the director of religious education in a parish in Wisconsin. She told us that every morning after her husband goes to work and the kids are off to school, she retires to a space in her home designated as a quiet place. There she prays a form of the Jesus Prayer for fifteen minutes. She said that when she is unable to fit this practice into her morning, her day never goes as well.

There are others whose daily Sabbaths are longer, a half hour or an hour. One of the things that came out about Joseph Cardinal Bernardin after his death was that for him, the first hour of every morning was a time of prayer. He admitted that sometimes it was mostly an hour of distractions; nevertheless, he gave the first hour of every day to God. Bernardin was our boss at the United States Catholic Conference during three years of our time there and we suspect that few, if any of us at the Conference, knew that he practiced a daily Sabbath. Weekly and daily Sabbaths provide a rest, a cessation from everyday work. It's something all of us need, including children.

In *Proclaim Jubilee*, Maria Harris tells us that Rabbi Abraham Heschel goes even further than simple cessation of work. On the Sabbath, he says, Jews are to resist even the thought of work. To illustrate this point, Heschel tells the story of a pious man who walks in his vineyard on the Sabbath and comes upon a fence with a breach that needs mending. "I shall fix that fence tomorrow," the man plans, "as soon as the Sabbath is over." But when the man prepares to do this at the end of the Sabbath, he changes his mind. "Since I thought of mending it on the Sabbath," he decides, "I shall never repair it."

Sabbath is a discipline of being in time. When we delve deeper into the meaning of Sabbath, it means more than just a length of time, such as three minutes, fifteen minutes, a half hour, an hour, twenty-four hours, six months, or a year. Sabbath acts as the religious summons to be present, the fully human mode of presence which is relationship to others.

Are We Present or Absent to Others?

Harris also refers to philosopher Gabriel Marcel, the twentieth century's greatest philosopher on the concept of presence. He writes that it is an undeniable fact of experience that some people fully offer us their presence; they are with us while others are not.

> Though it is hard to describe in intelligible terms, there are some people who reveal themselves as "present"—that is to say, at our disposal....There is a way of listening which is a way of giving, and another way of listening which is a way of refusing, of refusing oneself; the material gift, the visible action, do not necessarily witness to presence. We must not speak of proof in this connection; the word would be out of place. Presence is something which reveals itself in a look, a smile, an intonation, or a handshake.

Those common human experiences can teach us that the opposite of being present in time is neither living in the past nor living in the future. The opposite of being present is being absent.

John Shea's prayer poem "A Prayer for the Secret Solidarity of the Human Race," found in his book, *The Hour of the Unexpected*, pinpoints this kind of absence.

> The man I did not notice yesterday
>   died today
> And left me alone.

Many kids feel the awful vacuum of absence. On January 22, 2000, a fifteen-year-old-freshman at Gonzaga, the Jesuit high school in Washington, DC, where our godson is a student, hanged himself. We asked Miguel about this boy; we asked Billy, another student, about the boy; we asked others at Gonzaga about him; but nobody knew him. They never noticed him.

On April 6, 2000 a sixteen-year-old from Falls Church, Virginia, stopped his car at the east end of a local bridge, pounded several times on the hood of the vehicle, mounted the guardrail of an overpass, and dove off to his death. We will never know if this, too, was a case of being ignored but it is highly probable that something was going on in that young man's life that was missed, that was not seen.

In our everyday exchanges within our families, our workplaces, our classrooms, and in many other situations, our way of being present is a giving of ourselves or a refusal to give. Many times we are so preoccupied and encumbered with ourselves that there is little depth to our presence.

A good practice to check on our daily Sabbath presence is a nightly examen. Before we fall asleep we might ask, "How was I present to others during the day?" Sometimes what we discover will make us sad; other times, we'll feel glad. Many times it will be a mixture of both. The way we are present to others teaches about God's manner of presence in the world.

Stories that Highlight Presence and Absence

As Gabriel Marcel said, the kind of presence that is Sabbath-presence is hard to describe in intelligible terms. But we can capture its essence through story, story that describes a dynamic exchange in which something dramatic and saving occurs in the relationship. Here are some stories that do just that, as well as a few that highlight absence.

Presence
"Barrington Bunny," in *The Way of the Wolf*, by Martin Bell.
The Runaway Bunny, by Margaret Wise Brown.
Wilfrid Gordon McDonald Partridge, by Mem Fox.
"Mr. Entwhistle" and the poem "Hey World, Here I Am!" in *Hey World, Here I Am!* by Jean Little.
Sidewalk Story, by Sharon Bell Mathis.
Love You Forever, by Robert Munsch.

Absence
Terrible Things: An Allegory of the Holocaust, by Eve Bunting.
When Can Daddy Come Home? by Martha Whitmore Hickman.
Will Dad Ever Move Back Home? by Paula Z. Hogan.

Help Children Become Sabbath People

These are some ways to help children practice Sabbath.

1. Build pauses into your catechetical sessions. Name these moments of silence and quiet "Sabbath."

2. Show the children how to be really present to each other by simply listening when another is speaking. Call this "Sabbath presence."

3. Talk about Sunday as a day to rest and call this "practicing Sabbath."

4. Connect the practice of resting on Sunday with the commandment, "Remember to keep holy the Sabbath day."

5. Teach the children ways to practice "mini-Sabbaths," like praying the "Jesus prayer" during the day. A simple way to say this prayer is to first, be quiet enough so that we become conscious of our breathing. Then say the name, "Jesus" as we inhale and exhale.

6. Help the children to connect being still with Sabbath practice, and to sense that becoming still can often help them to know what to do or make a wise decision. A good story about this is "The Still," (anonymous), in *Sower's Seeds Aplenty* (Cavanaugh).

> When disaster strikes on a British naval vessel, a signal called "The Still" is sounded. This signal means "Stop what you're doing. Pause. Check your situation. Prepare to do the wise thing." Before the signal is sounded, few sailors know what is the wise thing to do. During the pause they learn what it is.
>
> We too run into emergencies in daily life. We too don't know what to do immediately. We cry out, "What can we do?" Actually the best thing we can do is to pause and be still. Pausing often spells the difference between success and failure.

For Your Reflection & Response

• If you don't already practice Sabbath you may want to start building it into your life. With other members of your faculty, plan times when you might pause during class time. Use each other as a support group. Report back during subsequent meetings and learn from each other how to be successful. Use books to help you, like:

Meditations on Silence, by Sister Wendy Beckett.

The Characters Within, by Joy Clough.

Laughter, Silence, and Shouting, by Kathy Keay. On page 17 of this book, she includes a traditional Celtic way to prepare for prayer:

I weave a silence on my lips,

I weave a silence into my mind,

I weave a silence within my heart.

I close my ears to distractions,

I close my eyes to attentions,

I close my heart to temptations.

Healing the Purpose of Your Life, by Dennis Linn, Sheila Fabricant Linn, and Matthew Linn.

Time Out in Shekina, by Catherine McCann.

Meditations, by Thomas Moore. Here you'll find this brief reflection, titled "Before Prayer":

Calm me O Lord as you stilled the storm,

Still me O Lord, keep me from harm.

Let all the tumult in me cease,

Enfold me Lord in your peace.

• Stop everything you are doing and read a wonderful piece of children's literature, *Out of the Dust*, by Karen Hesse. It won the John Newbery Medal.

Advent: Preparing for Christ's Coming

Advent is a four-week season. It begins on the Sunday closest to November 30 and ends on Christmas Day. It is a time of joyful expectation as we wait for Christ to come into our lives.

Expectation and waiting are symbolized in the Advent wreath. The base of the wreath is usually made of fresh evergreens that encircle three purple candles and a pink one. On the first Sunday of Advent, one of the purple candles is lit and a special prayer is said. On the second Sunday, a second purple candle is lit along with the first one, and another prayer is said. The pink candle is lit on the third Sunday, traditionally called Gaudete Sunday. It expresses a joyful note of anticipation within the season. The lighting of the fourth candle on the Sunday before Christmas heralds the final moments of waiting.

Lighting of the Advent wreath is an important ritual for children. We found this out one year while catechizing a group of sixth graders in Cheverly, Maryland. The religious ed classes were held on Sunday. On the first Sunday of Advent that year we decided that we wouldn't have a class Advent wreath as we usually did, because there was a beautiful one in the church. Big mistake!

On the second Sunday of Advent we were out of town, so the teacher of another group of sixth graders included our class with his. When we returned on the third Sunday of Advent, the children asked why we didn't have an Advent wreath in our class. They talked lovingly about what had happened with the wreath in the other teacher's session. They were obviously disappointed that we didn't have an Advent wreath, and missed its significant symbol and ritual. Our excuse for not having one ultimately sounded lame, even to us.

Part of the challenge of Advent is finding ways to involve the children's religious imagination in understanding expectancy and waiting. One of the more successful things we've done is invite mothers and fathers who are expecting a baby to visit our class. The parents come prepared to share their stories, which may include telling the class how long they've been waiting for this child, how much they have longed for the child, or what they plan to do as a couple or family to welcome the child. Then we read aloud *Everett Anderson's Nine Months Long,* by Lucille Clifton, or *The Baby Sister,* by Tomie dePaola.

After hearing stories of waiting from expectant parents and from children's literature, we give the children opportunities to remember and tell stories about their own experiences of waiting. We also reflect together on how hard it is sometimes to wait, but also, how waiting can help us to grow up a bit.

Unselfish Giving and Action in Advent
Advent reflects the longing for the birth of Jesus that occurred centuries ago. Advent also guides us to look for Christ's "second coming" at the end of the world. But Advent's most immediate longing is for the coming of the Risen Christ in our own lives.

One of the most important things we can do with children during Advent is to develop their capacity for generosity and unselfish behavior. We can do this by helping them make the connection between the coming of Christ into the world and their presence in the world as his followers. Involving the children in practical, hands-on activities is a good way to reinforce this connection.

In our parish, a "toy Sunday" is held before Christmas. Children, with their families, purchase new toys and/or choose from the toys they already own, and bring them to the children's Mass on a designated Sunday in Advent. As bicycles, tricycles, dolls, musical instruments, books, games, doll houses, and other treasures are carried up to the sanctuary, the difficulty of parting with some of the stuff is evident in some of the children. Occasionally there are tears as a child returns without a precious toy. In one instance, a little girl reluctantly and gently placed her doll near the other toys, started to return to her place, paused momentarily, turned around, picked up her doll, and hugged it all the way back to her seat.

When all the toys are placed near the altar, the sanctuary is filled with a wondrous array of gifts. These are a powerful sign to the community of children giving to other children who are much needier than they.

The "giving tree" is another activity in which both parents and children participate. Together, they take paper ornaments that have been hung on large evergreen trees which stand near both of the side entrances. Written on each paper ornament is a gift suggestion for an item that can be used by a needy adult. On the Sunday closest to Christmas, the gifts are put under the tree and later distributed to places like local prisons, homeless shelters, or halfway houses.

Some families also choose another family and give gifts to each member, as well as provide them with a complete Christmas dinner. And some families invite a single person, a couple, or a family who would have nowhere else to go to join them at their Christmas meal.

There are many creative ways to nurture a spirit of generosity and unselfish behavior during Advent, giving this season great meaning and making the wait a time of joy.

Stories that Reveal the Advent Spirit
Stocking children's imaginations with stories of generosity is a tried and true way of initiating them into the spirit of preparation that is the mark of the Advent season.

The following story might be read to children at the beginning of Advent to give them ideas of things that might be done together to help the poor in your neighborhood and community. Do not be afraid to challenge and encourage children to embody a selfless and generous spirit. The story is "The Face in the Window," (anonymous), found in *The Sower's*

Seeds (Cavanaugh).

It was Christmas Eve. A jostling crowd of shoppers was busy grabbing last-minute bargains. A small girl in tattered clothes made her way through the crowd. Her name was Nelly. You will find such a girl in your city or town if you will look around.

Nelly was also shopping—window shopping. She had no money and she was hungry. The twinkling lights, the colorful Christmas candles, the dazzling decorations and displays in the shop windows fascinated Nelly. As she passed the bakery with the cakes and pastries, she felt even more hungry. She paused...then moved a step closer to press her little snub nose against the window as she gazed at the Christmas "goodies." It lasted only a while. The manager saw the face in the window—the pale face pinched with hunger—so Nelly was told gruffly: "You there, be off!"

Nelly did not need a second bidding. She was frightened. She hurried through the crowd until she reached the attic where she lived with her aged grandma. Grandma was asleep. Sleep was the only thing they did not have to buy. This was the slumber that helped them forget misfortune—being hungry, no gifts, no new clothes, no decorations. Nelly also soon found refuge in sleep. From the distance wafted the strains of the well-loved carol: "Hark, the herald angels sing."

Is there such a Nelly in your neighborhood with whom you can share the joys and blessings of Christmas? All you have to do is look around.

The story that follows, *With Love at Christmas*, by Mem Fox, is so much of a favorite with children that they usually want to hear it more than once.

There once was an old Italian woman called Mrs. Cavallaro who had lived in her neighborhood most of her life. Her husband had died some years before. Among her friends and relations she was well known for her kindness and generosity, especially at Christmas.

Every year, as early as October, Mrs. Cavallaro began her shopping. In the smart shops and the craft shops, in the markets and the malls she bought presents for everyone she knew—her children and her grandchildren, her other relations and all her friends, everyone, that is, except her older grandsons to whom she gave money.

"They wouldn't be happy with socks or handkerchiefs," she thought.

By the end of November she had wrapped every present, and on each gift tag she had written, *"With love, at Christmas."*

She kept all her presents in a large wooden chest in her bedroom, and long before Christmas, her younger grandchildren would plead with her to let them look inside.

"Only a little peep, Grandma. Please!"

But her eyes just twinkled and she kept the chest firmly closed. One year, close to Christmas, news came to Mrs. Cavallaro of a terrible famine in Africa.

"What can I do to help?" she wondered. "I have no money left. I have spent it all on Christmas presents."

Hardly realizing what she was doing, she took the money she had intended for her grandsons and mailed it away to buy food for the hungry.

A few mornings later in the newspaper, she read about a family of nine, so poor that they could not afford presents for Christmas.

Hardly realizing what she was doing, she packed up the toys she had intended for her younger grandchildren and sent them to the family who would otherwise have had none.

Just before Christmas, the husband of one of her neighbors was hurt in an accident at work.

"He may never work again," cried the neighbor. "How shall we live?"

Hardly realizing what she was doing, Mrs. Cavallaro gathered the gifts of clothing and linen intended for her children, took them to the neighbor's house, and left them on the porch.

And so it happened that on Christmas Eve the wooden chest was empty. When she realized what she had done, Mrs.Cavallaro broke down and wept.

"What shall I do? Now I have nothing left to give to my family. The chest is empty and so is my purse."

When she went to bed that night she tossed and turned for a long time before she fell asleep. Not long after midnight, she was awakened by a small cry coming from the direction of the wooden chest. As she arose and went over to it, a beautiful light filled the room, and there, lying on a bed of straw, was a baby. She knelt before the child and brushed the straw from his face.

On Christmas morning, Mrs. Cavallaro was found dead, kneeling at her wooden chest. The baby was nowhere to be seen.

"Oh, no!" cried her family. "She was taking out our presents to put them under the tree."

For it is true that the chest which had been empty was once again filled with gifts, and on each one was written... *"With love, at Christmas."*

Another story that fascinates children is, "The Christmas Shell," adapted by Gerald Horton Bath in *Sower's Seeds Aplenty: Fourth Planting* (Cavanaugh). This story gently suggests that what we put into a gift is part of its value, part of the sacrifice.

A missionary was visiting several islands in the South Pacific before Christmas. He had been telling his native students how Christians, as an expression of their joy, gave one another presents on Christ's birthday.

On Christmas morning, one of the natives brought the missionary a seashell of lustrous beauty. When asked where he had discovered such an extraordinary shell, the native said he walked many miles to a certain bay—the location where such shells can be found.

"I think," exclaimed the missionary with gratitude, "it was wonderful of you to travel so far to get this lovely gift for me."

His eyes brightening, the native answered, "Long walk part of the gift!"

Poetry

A poem that expresses the kind of attitude and behavior that we hope children will always connect with Advent and the other days of their lives is, "The Joy of Giving," by John Greenleaf Whittier, which can be found in *The Family Read-Aloud Christmas Treasury*, selected by Alice Low.

> Somehow, not only for Christmas
>   But all the long year through,
> The joy that you give to others
>   Is the joy that comes back to you;
>
> And the more you spend in blessing
>   The poor and lonely and sad,
> The more of your heart's possessing
>   Returns to make you glad.

Advent Stories in Children's Literature

The meaning of Advent can be found in many pieces of children's literature. A tiny sampling of those that we particularly like are:

Everett Anderson's Christmas Coming, by Lucille Clifton. Everett becomes more excited as each of the five days before Christmas goes by. In joyful text and glorious, colorful drawings the story of Everett's wait and the coming of Christmas is poignantly told.

Tell Me Again about the Night I Was Born, by Jamie Lee Curtis. In this book, a little girl who has been adopted asks to hear, again, about the night of her birth, how her parents went to get her, how they felt the first moment they saw her, and how, because of her, they became a family.

On the Day You Were Born, by Debra Frasier. This is an exquisitely worded and illustrated story of how the whole world awaited the birth of baby Calla, prepared for her arrival, and celebrated when she came. "We're so glad you've come!" are words that were lovingly sung into Calla's ear. And, on the final page Calla's mother holds her tightly in her arms as dancing people encircle them.

Maria, by Theodore Taylor. Maria, an eleven-year-old, painfully longs to have a float in the Christmas parade that is part of the Christmas celebration in the town of San Lazaro. So she enters her family's name. Unlike the wealthy ranchers, however, her Mexican-American family has neither money nor ideas for a beautiful float.

As the parade day approaches it doesn't seem likely that the Gonzaga family will have a float. Maria's disappointment and embarrassment grows. How the Gonzagas solve their problem in time provides a moving conclusion to a story of one girl's struggle to break through cultural and economic barriers, bringing into play the true spirit of Christmas.

The Christmas Miracle of Jonathan Toomey, by Susan Wojciechowski. This is a unique and special story about preparing for Christmas, in which a small boy and his widowed mother gently warm the sad heart of a woodcarver as he carves a Christmas crèche for them.

For Your Reflection & Response

• Reflect on your memories and feelings about the Advent season. What is one thing you particularly enjoy doing during Advent? What is one thing you would like to change to make the season better?

• Tell the children stories of some of the saints whose feasts are celebrated during the season, e.g.: November 30, St. Andrew the Apostle; December 3, St. Francis Xavier; December 4, St. John of Damascus; December 6, St. Nicholas; December 7, St. Ambrose; December 8, Feast of the Immaculate Conception; December 9, Blessed Juan Diego; December 13, St. Lucy; December 14, St. John of the Cross; December 21, St. Peter Canisius.

• Look through *Advent and Lent Activities for Children: Camels, Carols, Crosses, Crowns*, by Shiela Kielly and Sheila Geraghty, for suggestions for remembering, celebrating, and honoring the season.

10

Christmas: Celebrating the Incarnation

Christmas captures the imaginations of children and adults more than any other holy day or holiday. This feastday, the solemnity of the Incarnation, is second in liturgical importance only to the annual celebration of Easter. At Christmas, a feeling of expectancy fills the air and merry greetings abound. Long before the day arrives, lighted trees blossom on lawns and in town squares, stores, businesses, and homes. "Giving trees" sprout up near side entrances of churches.

Besides adding to the beauty of the season, the Christmas tree is an important and much loved symbol. Choosing a tree and decorating it often involve the whole family. Fir, spruce, and pine are the most popular Christmas trees; however, millions of American families today decorate fireproof artificial trees. Many others buy living trees and plant them in their yard or garden after Christmas, or give them to a park.

In spite of its dominant role at Christmastime, we have found that many children don't know any of the history or the legends connected to the Christmas tree. They are often surprised to discover that the first Christmas trees were not decorated as they are now. Here are three delightful stories about Christmas trees, found in the *Catholic Source Book*, by Peter Klein.

Christmas Tree, Fruit Tree
Medieval mystery plays employed fir trees decorated with apples to symbolize the Garden of Eden with its tree of life and forbidden fruit. Long after the mystery plays, the Germans remembered the tree, modifying its decoration by adding sacramental wafers along with the apples, to contrast the eating that brought death with the eating that brings life. As the decorations became more elaborate, the symbolism of the fall and redemption faded. Apples were joined by oranges and then brightly colored balls, while wafers became cookies cut in the shape of angels, stars, animals, and flowers.

St. Boniface and the Christmas Tree

St. Boniface was an eighth-century missionary, praised by Pope Gregory II, who brought Christianity to Germany. Returning to Germany later, he found that Christianity had not taken hold. On Christmas Eve he came upon the eldest son of the chieftain Gundhar being readied for sacrifice to the gods. The place was under the giant oak tree, sacred to their patron, Thor. Boniface, in order to prove these gods powerless, felled the tree with the stroke of an axe, to the astonishment of the onlookers.

When he was then asked for the word of God, Boniface proclaimed, "This is the word, and this is the counsel. Not a drop of blood shall fall tonight, for this is the birth night of the Saint Christ, son of the all-Father and savior of the world." Pointing to a nearby evergreen he continued, "This little tree, a young child of the forest, shall be a home tree tonight. It is the wood of peace, for your houses are built of fir. It is the sign of endless life, for its branches are ever green. See how it points toward heaven. Let this be called the tree of the Christ Child. Gather about it, not in the wild woods, but in your homes. There it will shelter no deeds of blood, but loving gifts and lights of kindness."

Luther and the Christmas Tree

A popular legend tells how Martin Luther, during a Christmas Eve walk, was inspired with the beauty of the starlit night sky. To reproduce the celestial wonder and to commemorate Christ's birth under the starry Bethlehem sky, Martin brought a fir tree to his home, decorated it with candles, and arranged beneath it the nativity.

This story has interesting resemblances to St. Boniface (the tree) and St. Francis (the first nativity scene with living people and animals).

One of our favorite stories about Christmas trees is *The Trees of the Dancing Goats*, by Patricia Polacco. A Jewish family, spared from an epidemic of scarlet fever, cuts down trees, decorates them, and puts them up in the houses of their Christian neighbors so they can celebrate Christmas. This is an unusually beautiful story because a family with a different religious background reaches out in respect and love to make sure that other families, their neighbors, can celebrate their belief in a traditional and time-honored way.

The Christmas Crèche

The crèche is another Christmas symbol that is much loved by both children and adults. We have collected crèches from different places we have visited, and we display them throughout our home during the Christmas season. We also use them to tell the Christmas story to children. Another name for the crèche is a Nativity set.

A crèche or Nativity set contains figures of Mary, Joseph, the Christ Child, shepherds, sheep, and barn animals. The Christ Child is usually wrapped in "swaddling" clothes and is lying on a bed of straw. The Three Kings are added on the feast of the Epiphany. You'll often find a crèche or Nativity set beneath Christmas trees in homes and churches. The custom of using a Christmas crèche derives from a practice of Francis of Assisi begun around the year 1223, who celebrated Christmas in a barn with animals and straw.

The Nativity Story

Most children never tire of the story of the first

Christmas, whether from the Bible or from children's literature. They also love to hear the Christmas story told in a new way, such as the version that Janaan wrote for the Catholic News Service. It is called "Jacob and the Baby: A Christmas Miracle."

> Jacob watched as his older brother, David, and his sister, Hannah, helped the travelers to their rooms in the inn. Most of them were from Nazareth and had been traveling for several days. They were dusty, tired and hungry.
>
> Jacob wasn't able to help much because his right leg was badly crippled and he was smaller than most kids his age. He loved to listen to the stories that the travelers told his parents and the other guests. He wondered about the census that had brought so many of them to Bethlehem. He noticed, too, that his father was beginning to turn guests away because all the rooms were filled. Some of the people didn't seem to mind, but one couple looked sad and worried. Jacob heard the man tell his father that they had been looking for a room all over town.
>
> "Please," he said, "my name is Joseph. My wife, Mary and I are from Galilee. She is going to have a baby and needs to rest. If you have any space at all, please let us stay just for tonight."
>
> Jacob saw his father shake his head, but the man couldn't seem to move away. He hobbled over to get a closer look at the couple. When he got near them, he tripped on the donkey's strap and fell. Joseph reached down, picked him up and checked to see if he was all right. Jacob knew he wasn't hurt, but he felt embarrassed until he looked into Joseph's eyes and saw kindness that he hadn't seen often in people's eyes. Usually he was taunted and jeered by other kids. Most adults looked away when they noticed his twisted and crippled leg.
>
> Then he noticed that the woman was also looking at him with real concern.
>
> Suddenly, he thought of the small barn they had behind the inn. He quietly asked his father if the travelers could stay there. His father must have been thinking about that, too, because he said, "Jacob, if you will show them where the barn is and if they are willing to spend the night there, they are welcome to stay."
>
> Joseph looked at Jacob and then at his father and said, "Sir, we will be fine there. Thank you very much." He reached into his pocket for money to pay but Jacob's father said, "No, the place is yours for as long as you need it. There is no charge."
>
> As Jacob led Joseph and Mary to the barn, he felt a wonderful happiness. He could hardly believe his father had let him help. It was the first time that his father had trusted him with their guests.
>
> When they arrived at the barn, Jacob was afraid that Joseph wouldn't want to put Mary so close to the animals. The place also needed to be cleaned up a bit. But Mary was smiling happily and helped clean a place for them to sleep. Jacob, knowing they must be hungry, told them that he would get them some food. When he started back to the inn he met Hannah bringing the supper their mother had prepared for them. Jacob had never before realized how caring his family was.
>
> Hannah suggested that Jacob go back with her, so he said, "Good night." He promised to be back the next morning to see if they needed anything.

Early the next morning Jacob hobbled down to the barn. He knew as soon as he got close that something big was going on. Shepherds from the nearby fields were streaming through the barn door. Others were coming out with awe and joy on their faces.

As he worked his way into the barn he saw the baby. Joseph saw him come in and made a place for him near the makeshift crib.

Suddenly it seemed as though the baby looked directly at him. At the same moment Jacob felt something happening to his leg. He reached down to feel it. It was different from what it had been, but he wasn't sure what had happened. He tested it by putting his full weight on it. It didn't buckle.

For awhile Jacob felt like he couldn't move, but then he inched closer to the baby, fell on his knees, and found himself wondering who this child was and why his family had been chosen to open their hearts for his birth. Looking again into the baby's eyes he thanked the mysterious infant with joyful tears.

Again, as with stories of trees, there are many, many versions of the story of Jesus' birth. Many of them are set within particular cultures in which customs dictate the telling of the story. A favorite of ours is *The Night of Las Posadas*, by Tomie de Paola. The setting for this story is Santa Fe, New Mexico, where Christmas Eve is celebrated with the traditional procession called "Las Posadas." Sister Angie, who has been in charge of Las Posadas for years, arranges for the people of a nearby mountain village to re-enact Mary and Joseph's search for shelter on the night baby Jesus is born.

This year Las Posadas is going to be extra special because Sister Angie's niece, Lupe, and Lupe's husband, Roberto, are to play the parts of Mary and Joseph. But when Sister Angie becomes sick and Lupe and Roberto get stuck in a snowstorm, only a miracle can save Las Posadas. What happens to save the procession makes this a memorable and unforgettable Christmas story.

A beautiful book written in both Spanish and English, created by Charito Calvachi Wakefield, is *Navidad Latinoamericana/Latin American Christmas*. It contains Christmas traditions, hymns, prayers, and practices from twenty-five Latin American countries in both English and Spanish. It includes "La Novena de Navidad/Nine Days of Prayers before Christmas," as well as a CD.

Acting Out the Story of the Nativity

We believe that children should have an opportunity to help dramatize the Christmas story. We are aware that it is a challenge to put on a Nativity play, but it can be done. With some adult help, the children themselves can create a script by using the story of the birth of Jesus found in Luke's gospel, chapter two. There are also many books which offer simple playlets that can be drawn upon, like *The Story of Christmas*, retold by Anita Ganeri, or *Over 150 Easy-to-Use Gospel Plays for Children*, by Carol Camp Twork.

The value of giving children an opportunity to slip into the roles that make up the Christmas story is evident in the tale, "The Star," (anonymous), in *Sower's Seeds Aplenty: Fourth Planting* (Cavanaugh).

> The day of the Christmas pageant finally arrived. My niece, Kaitlin, was so excited about her part that I supposed she was one of the main characters, though she had not told me what her part was. The

parents were all there, and one by one the children took their places. I could see the shepherds fidgeting in the corner of the stage meant to represent the fields for the sheep. Mary and Joseph stood solemnly behind the manger. In the back, three young Wise Men waited impatiently. At the edge of the stage, Kait sat quietly and confidently.

Then the teacher began: "A long time ago, Mary and Joseph had a baby and they named him Jesus." She continued, "And when Jesus was born, a bright star appeared over the stable."

At that cue, Kait got up, picked up a large tinfoil star, walked behind Mary and Joseph and held the star up high for everyone to see.

When the teacher told about the shepherds coming to see the baby, the three young shepherds came forward, and Kait jiggled the star up and down excitedly to show them where to come. When the Wise Men responded to their cue, Kait went forward a little to meet them and lead the way. Her face was as brilliant as the original star must have been.

The playlet ended, followed by refreshments. On the way home Kait said with great satisfaction, "I had the main part."

"You did?" I questioned, wondering why she thought that.

"Yes," she said, "'cause I showed everybody how to find Jesus." How true! To show others how to find Jesus, to be the light for their paths—that is the finest role we can play in life.

Children's Own Stories of Christmas

One of the most interesting and rewarding things that we've done with children is giving them opportunities to write their own stories.

Because we invite, encourage, and challenge children to write in every one of our classes throughout the year, their ability to draw upon their imagination and experience grows. Some of their best stories have been written about Christmas. A favorite of ours is by Suzanne Schweiters, one of our former sixth graders at St. Luke's Parish in McLean, Virginia.

On December 25, 1982 a bratty, spoiled girl named Suzanne found out what Christmas was all about and that she should become a kind and loving person.

It all started on Christmas Eve at 8:00 pm just after Suzanne's mother tucked her in to bed. While all the other children were dreaming sweet Christmas dreams Suzanne was sticking her glow-in-the-dark skeleton out her window above, scaring the passing villagers. Then it happened. Angel Gabriel came over Suzanne's roof and said, "Suzanne, stop scaring the people!"

"Oh, put a lid on it," Suzanne retorted. "Who are you anyways?"

"I am the Angel Gabriel. I have come to teach you the true value of Christmas."

"You belong in a nut house with the squirrels!" Suzanne replied.

"Just come, my child," Gabriel said.

"Okay. Whatever you say, ah… ah…Gabe."

So Gabriel and Suzanne set off. Gabriel was taking Suzanne to the birth of Jesus. When they got there Suzanne was so stunned with amazement that she promised she would be good and with that she learned the true value of Christmas.

Suzanne's is an imaginative story but many children have written real-life stories close to their experience. Surprisingly, many of these stories reveal worries, troubles, and sadness.

One child wrote a story about his family's Christmas without his mother, who was in prison. Another child, whose parents are divorced, wrote about having to choose to spend Christmas with one parent or the other. One of the things that was most poignant in her story was that she said, "Choosing wasn't the hardest part. The hardest part was trying to feel happy while missing her other parent made her feel so unhappy."

Yet the story we found most painful was by the child who told of the Christmas her family spent in a homeless shelter after her father lost his job. Her story was the inspiration for a story that Janaan wrote for a Catholic News Service Christmas issue of the newsletter *Faith Alive*. The story is called "Sarah's Christmas Wishes."

> Sarah reread her essay. It wasn't bad but she hated the assignment because she didn't want to share with her new class what she wanted for Christmas. What did writing an essay like this have to do with social studies anyway? This was just another thing that she didn't like about her new school. If she had written what she really wanted for Christmas—like being back at her old school with her friends in her old neighborhood—then she was sure she wouldn't be feeling so lonely and unhappy.
>
> Another thing she hated about the assignment was that the teacher had told them that they would be reading their essays aloud during class. What if no one else wanted a Barbie doll? What if all of them thought she was weird for wanting the story book *Where the Red Fern Grows* because it's about a boy? What if she got the bike she wanted and had no friends to ride with? As she reread her essay again, her heart ached with more "What if" questions.
>
> The next morning when she boarded the bus she was still worried about sharing her Christmas wishes. However, Christmas was just a week away so she made herself feel better by remembering that soon there would be almost ten days when she wouldn't have to go to school.
>
> Sarah took her seat in the class and kept her eyes down. The only person who didn't seem like a stranger was Miss Brown, the teacher. And when she looked up, Miss Brown smiled at her before she directed the class to rearrange their chairs into a circle. This got noisy but somehow it made Sarah feel more relaxed.
>
> When they were seated again, Miss Brown announced that this was a special class because they would be sharing their Christmas wishes with each other. "And when we share like this," she said, "we can get to know each other better. Getting to know each other can help us to become more caring. That's what I hope happens today in this class because Christmas is a caring, sharing season—a time to celebrate the birth of Jesus who is remembered for how much he cared."
>
> Miss Brown then called on Annie to read her essay and it wasn't all that different from Sarah's. Sarah felt better immediately. Then Jett read his, followed by Miguel and Erin. When Angela started to read hers everyone became very quiet.
>
> "My Christmas essay is different, I'm afraid, because when I tried to name things that I would like for Christmas I knew my Dad wouldn't be able to buy them for me. He has been out of a job for three months now and is unsure when he will find another one. So what I want

more than anything else this Christmas is a job for my Dad."

As Sarah thought about what Angela had written, she decided that when her turn came, she would share what she really wanted for Christmas and maybe, just maybe her Dad might be able to help Angela's father.

Finally her turn came. She turned her paper over and looked at Miss Brown who nodded for her to begin.

"I wrote an essay which I've decided not to read because as I was listening to each of yours, I realized that the essay I wrote doesn't really tell what I want most for Christmas this year. I want a friend. I found it hard to leave my old school and friends but my Dad is starting a new company in this city and we had to move. Angela, I have another wish for Christmas—that your Dad will apply for a job in my Dad's company."

As Sarah finished her essay, everyone clapped. Miss Brown wiped a tear from her eyes and dismissed them with the loving greeting, "Merry Christmas."

Christmas Stories in Children's Literature

Children's lives will be enriched if their minds and hearts are filled with the legends and stories of Christmas. There are dozens of old Christmas stories along with many new ones that are published every year, so doing the above is not all that hard. The following are just a few of the stories we have used to fill the hearts and minds of our children during the Christmas season.

The Best Gift for Mom, by Lee Klein. Jonathan's father is dead. One evening after Jonathan has lied about his father's death, his Mom tells him about how his father died so he won't have to lie about it anymore. Then Jonathan remembers how his father used to put him to sleep when he was little. And, using that memory, he gives his mom a special Christmas gift.

Jacob's Gift, by Max Lucado. Jacob is a carpenter's apprentice in Rabbi Simeon's shop. The Rabbi announces to the boys that whoever builds the best project will work with him on the new synagogue. Jacob loves working with wood and feels that he just has to be selected. He thinks long and hard about what he will build and finally decides to build a new kind of animal feed trough. It is the best work he has ever done and tomorrow the Rabbi will select the best apprentice. But that night he becomes aware that there's a new baby in the stable near his father's inn without a place to sleep. How and why Jacob is selected even though he has given away his "work" makes for an unusually beautiful Christmas tale.

The Gift of the Magi, by O. Henry. This is a classic story of a young couple who are very poor. It's Christmas Eve and each wants to give the other a longed-for present. How they manage to buy the gifts is a story of amazing sacrifice and deep love. It is also a story with an ending that is both exquisite and touching.

Christmas Gif': An Anthology of Christmas Poems, Songs, and Stories Written By and About African Americans, compiled by Charlamae Hill Rollins. This book is especially precious to Janaan because when she was a parochial school teacher on Chicago's South Side in the early 1960s, Charlamae Rollins was the librarian in the children's section of the local library. Once a month she helped Janaan choose books for the children in her classes and was genuinely delighted that she was encouraging them to read, read, read! In this collection there are wonderful Christmas poems, including several by Charlamae's friend, Langston Hughes. Our favorite story in the collection is "The Legend of the Black Madonna," by Margaret T. Applegarth.

A Christmas Story, by Brian Wildsmith. This book is an original and enchanting presentation of the Nativity. Wildsmith's rich paintings with their brilliant colors and shining gold, reflect the miracle of the Christ child's birth and joyously celebrate its beauty.

The Best Gift of All, by Cornelia Wilkeshuis. Prince Irenus, the young son of King Balthasar, decides to follow the star, so he can also see the new Prince. He knows his father is taking a golden goblet as a gift so Irenus decides to take along his red bouncing ball, his favorite book, and his beloved dog, Pluton. He's not sure he'll be able to give up his pet but he sets out with that in mind. On the way he finds others who need his gifts and when he arrives at the stable, he has nothing left to give the Prince of Peace.

The above is a wonderful story for children to act out. One Christmas, as part of the homily, children at Our Lady Queen of Peace Church in Arlington, Virginia, dramatized the story to the congregation's inspiration and delight.

For Your Reflection & Response

• Remember Christmases past in your life. Pause long enough to plan for Christmas present.

• Take time to visit one or more of your local bookstores and become acquainted with the new Christmas stories or with old Christmas stories you have never read. Many will be pedestrian but usually there are some that are real gems. Make it a rule of thumb that if a story doesn't take you beyond where you are now, it will probably not do much for a child either. Choose carefully and share one or more of these stories with the children in your life.

• Page through a book like *Christmas Crafts and Customs Around the World*, by Virginia Fowler, or *Legends and Traditions of Christmas*, by Trudie West Revoir for activities that you may want to do with your children.

11

Lent: Observing with Prayer, Fasting, & Almsgiving

Many Catholics have vivid memories of the strict practices that once marked the season of Lent. For example, we remember fasting every day except Sundays and St. Patrick's Day, and attending lenten devotions in our parishes. We gave up things, mostly candy, and there was a penitential aura about the season. We could feel Lent in our bones. This feeling still lingers and continues to color Lent for us.

The Ash Wednesday ritual of applying blessed ashes on our foreheads was significant. Many of us wore proudly the black, cross-like mark throughout that day. The formula that was prayed while the ashes were applied was a grim reminder of who we essentially are—so much so that the words still come easily to mind: "Remember, man, that you are dust and unto dust you shall return."

Ash Wednesday is still a significant opening to Lent, and the above formula is still used; however, the one that is more frequently prayed today is, "Turn from sin and live the gospel."

Fasting

To turn from sin is to turn toward what is good, toward a more loving way of being in the world. Lent, therefore, is an ideal time to provide children with the kind of nurture that increases in them an emotional attachment to goodness. Story is a unique source of that kind of nurture. One that does this both powerfully and gently is Dan Clark's story "Puppies for Sale," from *Chicken Soup for the Soul*, by Jack Canfield and Mark Victor Hansen.

> A store owner was tacking a sign above his door that read "Puppies for Sale." Signs like that have a way of attracting small children, and sure enough, a little boy appeared under the store owner's sign. "How much are you going to sell the puppies for?" he asked.
>
> The store owner replied, "Anywhere

from $30 to $50."

The little boy reached in his pocket and pulled out some change. "I have $2.37," he said, "Can I please look at them?"

The store owner smiled and whistled and out of the kennel came Lady, who ran down the aisle of his store followed by five teeny, tiny balls of fur. One puppy was lagging considerably behind. Immediately the little boy singled out the lagging, limping puppy and said, "What's wrong with that little dog?"

The store owner explained that the veterinarian had examined the little puppy and had discovered it didn't have a hip socket. It would always limp. It would always be lame. The little boy became excited. "That is the little puppy that I want to buy."

The store owner said, "No, you don't want to buy that little dog. If you really want him, I'll just give him to you."

The little boy got quite upset. He looked straight into the store owner's eyes, pointing his finger, and said, "I don't want you to give him to me. That little dog is worth every bit as much as all the other dogs and I'll pay full price. In fact, I'll give you $2.37 now, and 50 cents a month until I have him paid for."

The store owner countered, "You really don't want to buy this little dog. He is never going to be able to run and jump and play with you like the other puppies."

To this the little boy reached down and rolled up his pant leg to reveal a badly twisted, crippled left leg supported by a big metal brace. He looked up at the store owner and softly replied, "Well, I don't run so well myself, and the little puppy will need someone who understands!"

Another story that is frequently read at soup suppers during Lent is *Stone Soup*, by Marcia Brown. It deals creatively and provocatively with turning from sin toward what is good, toward a more loving way of being in the world. This book has been around for a long time, and is available in most bookstores in both hardback and paperback editions.

There are many more stories that nurture an emotional attachment to goodness. Four that we recommend are:

Shiloh, by Phyllis Reynolds Naylor. A boy's willingness to do anything to save an abused dog from a cruel owner is a powerful story of goodness in a child. This story won the John Newbery Medal.

The Hundred Penny Box, by Sharon Bell Mathis. A small child is poignantly sensitive to what an elderly relative needs and does what he has to do to make sure it is not taken from her.

The Jade Stone, by Caryn Yacowitz. Chan Lo, a stone carver, disobeys the Great Emperor of all China, in spite of his fear of punishment, because he can't go against what he knows he has to do.

The Quiltmaker's Gift, by Jeff Brumbeau. A generous quiltmaker, with magic in her fingers, sews the most beautiful quilts in the world then gives them away. How she changes a greedy king who yearns for one of her quilts is at the heart of this story.

Prayer

Another lenten basic is praying. Some of the praying that is part of Lent arises out of the colors, the symbols, the food, the music, and the rituals. Helping children to experience these elements brings them into touch with Lent's spirit and meaning.

In our parish, two penitential symbols dramatically inspire a prayerful response. On Ash Wednesday, a long swatch of sackcloth is hung behind the huge, austere wooden cross above the altar. Another piece of sackcloth covers the altar table. The fabric, along with the ashes from Ash Wednesday, help us to remember Lent has begun.

Several years ago we were catechists to fifth and sixth grade children at Our Lady Queen of Peace Parish in South Arlington, Virginia. We met weekly around a large table in the parish's main meeting room. On the first Sunday of Lent we covered the table with a purple cloth and placed on it a large crucifix and and a bowl of pretzels. We invited the children to talk about each item.

The children didn't know the pretzel legend, so we told them this story: according to the legend, monks originated the pretzel during the Middle Ages. They formed dough into shapes that resembled arms folded in prayer, baked the pretzels, then gave them out to children as a reward for learning their prayers.

On some of the Sundays during Lent we brought in hot cross buns as a treat. They, too, are a lenten food made out of sweetened dough filled with raisins and dried fruit and topped with a cross made out of white frosting.

Using items and symbols that involve the senses can help children enter into the spirit of Lent and thus deepen their prayer life. Reading stories about prayer can also help. One that we like is "A Grandfather's Prayer," by Barry Lopez, from *Sower's Seeds Aplenty: Fourth Planting*.

> One drizzly morning Barry got up and went off alone, before breakfast, for a walk in the woods. As he squished through the pines and cedars, he recalled a similar morning in his youth when he saw his grandfather go off alone through the same woods. When his grandfather returned, little Barry asked him where he had been and what he had done out there.
>
> His grandfather smiled, put his arm around Barry and said, "Let's go get some breakfast."
>
> As Barry continued to walk in the drizzle, he came to a clearing in the woods. There he knelt down and placed his hands flat against the damp earth. It gave him a feeling of being united with all creation. Barry recalled how his grandfather told him that if he ever felt lonely, he should go for a walk in the woods, be quiet, and do whatever he felt moved to do, like kneeling down and placing his hands flat against the earth.
>
> Half an hour later when Barry started back to the cabin, he felt renewed. He felt recharged. Then he remembered his grandfather used to walk in the woods in the morning twilight. Barry's grandmother once told him it was the way his grandfather said his prayers. He would always end up on the other side of the woods, standing on the beach with his hands in his pockets, listening to the ocean.

Another story from the same book that we've also read in our sessions is "More To Life," by Grant Teaff:

> Coach Grant Teaff, in his book *I Believe*, describes an incident that happened early in his career at McMurray College. One Saturday night he and his team had just taken off in a chartered plane for the return to Texas. Suddenly the plane developed serious engine problems. The pilot announced that he would have to attempt an emergency landing. The plane was loaded with fuel, so an explosion also was likely.

As the plane sped downward, one of the players called out, "Coach Teaff, would you lead us in prayer? We're all pretty frightened." Teaff prayed out loud so everyone could hear.

Seconds later, the plane bellied across the runway. A shower of sparks engulfed the plane. Miraculously, however, it did not explode, and no one was hurt.

The next night Teaff and his family were in church together. Right in the middle of the service, Teaff got up, left the church, and went to the McMurray Fieldhouse about a mile away. He went straight to the team's dressing room and knelt down and prayed:

God, I know that you have a plan, a purpose, and a will for my life and the lives of these young men. I do not know what it is, but I'll try to impress upon the young men that there is more to life than just playing football, that you do have a purpose for their lives.

We have found both of these stories helpful because they provoke questions like, "Who did Barry and his grandfather pray to when they were out in the woods?" "Can you pray without saying anything?" "Why didn't Coach Teaff stay in church to say his prayer?" They also prompt the children to recall stories of praying from their own lives.

During Lent we always like to pray the Way of the Cross with the children we teach. A book that we have used again and again as a guide is *A Bible Way of the Cross for Children*, by Gwen Costello. We have also had children make their own version of each of the stations and have used these versions to walk the Way of the Cross

Poetry can also help children deepen their sense of prayer. The poem, "When I Want To Pray," by Christy Kenneally in *Miracles and Me*, is good for doing that.

When I want to pray
I don't put on a face
Or search for a desert
Or other such place
I can pray at my ease
Any place I can find,
Whether sitting or kneeling.
The Lord doesn't mind.

When I want to pray
I don't talk about me
And weary the Lord
With how good I can be.
I close up my mouth
And open my ears
To the love of the Lord
That will banish my fears.

When I want to pray
I don't try to impress.
If I haven't been loving
I'm quick to confess.
And I know that the Lord
Who made birds in the sky,
Who cares for the tiniest
Sparrows that fly,
Who never stops caring
By night or by day,
Will hear me and love me
Whenever I pray.

Almsgiving
Almsgiving is another lenten basic. Essentially it means reaching out to the poor, the sick, and the needy. Children are easily inspired to this practice, partially through opportunities to do it with others, partially through being around adults who do it, and partially through the nurture of stories in which the characters act compassionately and generously. Planted

in the hearts and minds of children, these stories can become the seeds of almsgiving.

One such story is "Heroes" (anonymous), from the book *The Sower's Seeds* (Cavanaugh).

Babe Ruth had hit 714 home runs during his baseball career and was playing one of his last full major league games. It was the Braves vs. the Reds in Cincinnati. But the great Bambino was no longer as agile as he had been. He fumbled the ball and threw badly, and in one inning alone his errors were responsible for most of the five runs scored by Cincinnati.

As the Babe walked off the field and headed toward the dugout after the third out, a crescendo of yelling and booing reached his ears. Just then a boy jumped over the railing onto the playing field. With tears streaming down his face, he threw his arms around the legs of his hero.

Ruth didn't hesitate for a second. He picked up the boy, hugged him, and set him down on his feet, patting his head gently. The noise from the stands came to an abrupt halt. Suddenly there was no more booing. In fact, a hush fell over the entire park. In those brief moments, the fans saw two heroes: Ruth, who, in spite of his dismal day on the field, could still care about a little boy; and the small boy who cared about the feelings of another human being. Both had melted the hearts of the crowd.

Another story that melts the hearts of young and old is "The Visit," by Debbie Herman, found in *Chicken Soup for the Kid's Soul*.

Every Saturday, Grandpa and I walk to the nursing home a few blocks away from our house. We go to visit many of the old and sick people who live there because they can't take care of themselves anymore.

"Whoever visits the sick gives them life," Grandpa always says.

First we visit Mrs. Sokol. I call her "The Cook." She likes to talk about the time when she was a well-known cook back in Russia. People would come from miles around, just to taste her famous soup.

Next we visit Mr. Meyer. I call him "The Joke Man." We sit around his coffee table, and he tells us jokes. Some are very funny. Some aren't. And some I don't get. He laughs at his own jokes, shaking up and down and turning red in the face. Grandpa and I can't help but laugh along with him, even when the jokes aren't very funny.

Next door is Mr. Klipman. I call him "The Singer" because he loves to sing for us. Whenever he does, his beautiful voice fills the air, clear and strong and so full of energy that we always sing along with him.

We visit Mrs. Kagan, "The Grandmother," who shows us pictures of her grandchildren. They're all over the room, in frames, in albums and even taped to the walls.

Mrs. Schreiber's room is filled with memories, memories that come alive as she tells us stories of her own experiences during the old days. I call her "The Memory Lady."

Then there's Mr. Krull, "The Quiet Man." He doesn't have very much to say; he just listens when Grandpa or I talk to him. He nods and smiles, and tells us to come again next week. That's what everyone says to Grandpa and me, even the woman in charge, behind the desk.

Every week we do come again, even in

the rain. We walk together to visit our friends: The Cook, The Joke Man, The Singer, the Grandmother, the Memory Lady and The Quiet Man.

One day Grandpa got very sick and had to go to the hospital. The doctors said they didn't think he would ever get better.

Saturday came, and it was time to visit the nursing home. How could I go visiting without Grandpa? Then I remembered what Grandpa once told me: "Nothing should stand in the way of doing a good deed." So I went alone.

Everyone was happy to see me. They were surprised when they didn't see Grandpa. When I told them that he was sick and in the hospital, they could tell I was sad.

"Everything is in God's hands," they told me. "Do your best and God will do the rest."

The Cook went on to reveal some of her secret ingredients. The Joke Man told me his latest jokes. The Singer sang a song especially for me. The Grandmother showed me more pictures. The Memory Lady shared some of her memories. When I visited The Quiet Man, I asked him lots of questions. When I ran out of questions, I talked about what I had learned in school. After a while, I said good-bye to everyone, even the woman in charge, behind the desk.

"Thank you for coming," she said. "May your grandfather have a complete recovery."

A few days later, Grandpa was still in the hospital. He was not eating, he could not sit up and he could barely speak. I went to the corner of the room so Grandpa wouldn't see me cry. My mother took my place by the bed and held Grandpa's hand. The room was dim and very quiet.

Suddenly the nurse came into the room and said, "You have some visitors."

"Is this the place with the party?" I heard a familiar voice ask.

I looked up. It was The Joke Man. Behind him were The Cook, The Singer, The Grandmother, The Memory Lady, The Quiet Man and even the woman in charge, behind the desk.

The Cook told Grandpa about all the great food that she would cook for him once he got well. She had even brought him a hot bowl of homemade chicken soup.

"Chicken soup? What this man needs is a pastrami sandwich," said The Joke Man as he let out one of his deep rich laughs.

Everyone laughed with him. Then he told us some new jokes. By the time he was finished, everyone had to use tissues to dry their eyes from laughing so hard.

Next, The Grandmother showed Grandpa a get-well card made by two of her granddaughters. On the front of one card was a picture of a clown holding balloons. "Get well soon" was scribbled in crayon on the inside.

The Singer started singing, and we all sang along with him. The Memory Lady told us how Grandpa once came to visit her in a snowstorm just to bring her some roses for her birthday.

Before I knew it, visiting hours were up. Everyone said a short prayer for Grandpa. Then they said good-bye and told him that they would see him again soon.

That evening, Grandpa called the nurse in and said he was hungry. Soon he began to sit up. Finally he was able to get out of bed. Each day, Grandpa felt better and better, and he grew stronger and stronger. Soon he was able to go home.

The doctors were shocked. They said his recovery was a medical miracle. But I knew the truth: his friends' visit had made him well.

Grandpa is better now. Every Saturday, without fail, we walk together to visit our friends: The Cook, The Joke Man, The Singer, The Grandmother, The Memory Lady, The Quiet Man…and the woman in charge, behind the desk.

Another story that speaks to lenten almsgiving is "Big Feet—Bigger Heart," (anonymous), in *Sower's Seeds Aplenty: Fourth Planting* (Cavanaugh).

> It was an unseasonably hot day. Everybody, it seemed, was looking for some kind of relief, so an ice cream store was a natural place to stop.
>
> A little girl, clutching her money tightly, came into the store. Before she could say a word, the store clerk sharply told her to get outside and read the sign on the door, and stay out until she put on some shoes. She left slowly, and a big man followed her out of the store.
>
> He watched as she stood in front of the store and read the sign: No Bare Feet. Tears started to roll down her cheeks as she turned and started to walk away. Just then the big man called to her. Sitting down on the curb, he took off his size 12 shoes, and set them in front of the girl, saying, "Here. You won't be able to walk in these, but if you sort of slide along, you can get your ice cream cone."
>
> Then he lifted the little girl up, and set her feet into the shoes. "Take your time," he said. "I get tired of moving them around, and it'll feel good to just sit here and eat my ice cream." The shining eyes of the little girl could not be missed as she shuffled up to the counter and ordered her ice cream cone.
>
> He was a big man, all right. Big belly, big shoes, but, most of all, he had a big heart.

More Stories of Caring People

Stories about saints and other people who cared and care, in a radical way, for the poor, the sick, and the dying provide models and inspiration for living out this lenten basic.

A recent book, *All Saints*, by Robert Ellsberg, is an excellent resource for stories of "saints, prophets, and witnesses for our time." What is remarkable about the book is that, while there are many already canonized saints featured, the majority are people who have not yet been recognized as saints by the church, but who lived lives of remarkable goodness. These include Dorothy Day, Mother Teresa of Calcutta, Pope John XXIII (whose causes for beatification and canonization are being considered), Catherine de Hueck Doherty, Albert Schweitzer, Dom Helder Camara, James "Guadalupe" Carney (a contemporary of Carl's), and Felix and Mary Barreda.

One of the greatest gifts that we can give children during Lent is the desire to give themselves as is suggested in the poem, "Give Yourself" in the book *Miracles and Me*, by Christy Kenneally.

> When Old Mrs. Hennessy
> Opened the door,
> Susan saw parcels
> And cards on the floor.
>
> "It's my birthday,"
> The old lady said

With a smile.
"I'm here all alone.
Can you stay
For a while?"

And later while talking
She grew very sad.
"Now this is the eightieth
Birthday I've had.

Every year I get parcels
Piled up in the hall.
But rather than parcels
I'd love them to call.

I know you've worked hard
At your lessons all day.
I'm sure you'd prefer
To go out and play.

I have beautiful cards
In a line on the shelf.
But your present was nicest.
You gave me yourself."

**Helping Children
Enter into the Spirit of Lent**

• In many parishes families place a "rice bowl" in the center of the table during Lent. Money that is saved through sacrifice is placed in the bowl, returned to the parish on a given Sunday, then distributed among various programs that help feed the hungry. You might encourage this practice or something similar as part of classes during Lent.

• Every time you meet with the children do something with them that renews their awareness of Lent: that it begins on Ash Wednesday and ends on Holy Saturday; that fasting, prayer and almsgiving are the three hallmarks of the season; that the season has special colors, foods, symbols, rituals, music, and prayers.

• Besides the "rice bowl," involve the children in doing an action to help people in need in your community. Some ideas are conducting a clothing drive, stocking a food pantry with canned goods, or collecting story books to stock the library of a school in a depressed area.

For Your Reflection & Response

• This might be a good time to recall memories that you have of how you observed Lent during your childhood. Are there any experiences that you would like to build into the lives of the children you work with?

• Choose one thing that you personally will do this Lent that concerns prayer, one thing that concerns fasting, and one thing that concerns almsgiving. Try to make each of these practices something that you have never done before.

12

Easter: Celebrating Christ's Resurrection

Easter is the greatest feast of the church year. It celebrates the rising of Jesus Christ from the dead and is often referred to as the "feast of the Resurrection." It is a springtime feast, one associated with new life. Green grass, budding trees, blooming forsythia, daffodils, tulips, dogwood trees, and cherry blossoms are all part of Eastertime. New clothes and Easter bonnets add color and joy to what is referred to as "putting on new life."

In his book, *What Is God?* Joseph F. Girzone writes, "God is life in the earth that gives renewal to all creation in the springtime." Easter, more than any other feast, renews belief in a faith community. Some of that truth is expressed in a poem, titled "Resurrection," that Janaan wrote about the feast.

Into the
breezeless,
too dark
day
A huge
cloud
hovered, dipped and
broke
thunderously,
Spilling water
and jagged
flashes of light
into our scared
Selves
Causing the wind to blow,
the sun to shine, and
our hearts to believe.

Easter brushes up so close to Lent that most of the celebration of it occurs on the feastday itself and during the fifty days afterwards, the time known as the Easter season.

Easter Eggs

Coloring eggs is a favorite activity for children in preparation for Easter. Janaan's family religiously colored eggs on Holy Saturday afternoon—twelve dozen of them! The colored eggs were eaten on Easter and during the Easter season. They were also given as gifts and used as decorations.

Even more memorable than the boiling of the eggs, the coloring, and decorating of them was the happiness that came from relief that Good Friday was over, Lent had ended, and Jesus was in the tomb but he wasn't going to stay there. Janaan's family talked about all of this as they colored eggs, and ate the hardened candy which they had saved but not eaten during Lent. They also ate eggs whose shells had cracked, either while they were being boiled or decorated.

In *The Catholic Source Book*, by Peter Klein, there is this information about Easter eggs.

Easter caskets

Easter eggs are an important part of the celebration of Easter because they symbolize not only spring's rebirth, but also Christ's resurrection. Like the tomb, the egg is the hard, cold casket from which new life finally and triumphantly breaks forth. The Roman proverb *Omne vivum ex ovo* ("All life comes from an egg") took on a new, religious significance.

Lent's over

In Germany, eggs became part of the Easter decoration and celebration of the nineteenth century. If it was not its tempting symbolism that gave the egg a place in the Church, it was simply the food that it was: eggs were prohibited during Lent, and allowed again at Easter, so at very least they symbolized the end of the fast.

Colored Eggs

According to a Ukrainian folktale, a poor peddler went to the marketplace one day to sell a basket of eggs. He encountered a crowd mocking a man who was staggering under a heavy cross on which he was about to be crucified. Running to his aid, the peddler left the basket by the roadside. Upon his return, he found the eggs wondrously transformed with exquisite designs of bright colors. The man was Christ; the peddler, Simon of Cyrene; and the eggs were to become the symbol of rebirth for all humankind. Even today in the Ukraine, decorating *pysanky*, as the native eggs are called, is a treasured craft and custom.

Yosef's Gift of Many Colors, by Cassandre Maxwell, is an Easter story set in the Ukraine in which the custom and craft of decorating *pysanky* is featured. It is too long to include here but it's a near perfect story of decorating an Easter egg.

We have discovered that today many children don't experience the coloring of eggs in their families, so we often color eggs with them during the last class before Easter. While they are coloring the eggs we read stories to the children like the one named above, or *Rechenka's Eggs*, by Patricia Polacco.

You can find out more about customs surrounding Easter eggs in *Catholic Customs and Traditions*, by Greg Dues.

Other Easter Symbols

Other symbols that are part of Easter are the Paschal candle, Easter fire, Easter rabbit, Easter basket, and water that is blessed during the Easter Vigil and used throughout the Easter season.

The Easter season is a good time to acquaint children and young people with these symbols, especially the Paschal candle. They see this symbol in the sanctuary area of the church during the fifty days following Easter and throughout the rest of the liturgical year. If they attend the Easter Vigil they will see it blessed and lighted as a symbol of the risen Jesus of Nazareth, the Light of the World.

Inserted into the candle, in the form of a cross, are five grains of incense, which represent the five wounds of Jesus. The current year is cut into the candle to remind the faithful that the risen Christ is with them today.

For information about Easter bunnies and baskets, see the *Catholic Source Book*, by Peter Klein, *Advent and Lent Activities for Children: Camels, Carols, Crosses, Crowns*, by Shiela Kielly and Sheila Geraghty, and *Lilies, Rabbits, and Painted Eggs*, by Edna Barth.

Easter Fire
New fire is used to light the Paschal candle during the Easter Vigil on Holy Saturday. It is an important symbol because the light from the new fire banishes the darkness associated with Lent and is a stirring sign that Christ, the Light of the World, is risen, is alive, and is with us here and now.

There is no better way to introduce children to the significance of the Easter fire than with story, especially *Stepka and the Magic Fire*, by Dorothy VanWoerkom.

> In the days of the Tsars, on a hill above the Don River, was a certain poor village. No one in the village had very much in those days.
>
> The wars of Tsar Ivan the Terrible had ruined nearly all of Russia. The land had failed and the harvests were bad. Towns could no longer pay their taxes. Roaming bands of Cossacks frightened the peasants, and stole from them.
>
> But the family of Stepka had least of all. Stepka and his three small daughters lived on brown bread and water from the New Year to the Nativity.
>
> Still when Easter arrived on the high winds of late March, the village people tried to make the best of it. On Easter Eve they brought out precious sacks of flour for cakes and cookies. They ate cabbage soup and salted cucumbers and tea with lemon in it. After dark they lit their homes with Easter candles. And in every house but Stepka's there was fire against the cold March wind.
>
> At midnight neighbors ran from house to house. They carried torches to light their way. They wore bright smiles above their feastday clothes. With shouts and laughter they called the Easter greeting to each other.
>
> "Christ is risen!" they cried. And, "He is risen indeed!"
>
> Stepka did not join the others. He put his hungry children to bed with a song on his lips, with a pain in his heart. Long after they had fallen asleep he watched them as they lay huddled together on their cot. Tomorrow's breakfast would be more brown bread. But tomorrow was Easter!
>
> For Easter, at least, they should have something special.
>
> From a cupboard Stepka took a box of old Easter candles. He counted them out on the table. He longed to place them about the house and light them, to wake the children and watch their faces glow with pleasure. Only there was no fire in his house with which to light them. And he had no wood to make one.
>
> Now Stepka was a man too proud to beg. But just this once—for the children—he would do it. He hurried down the hill and through the village to beg

some fire from his neighbors.

"Give me a light for my Easter candles, good neighbor," he cried again and again. "A light for the love of heaven!"

"Be gone!" they told him.

"Take better care of your affairs, neighbor," they shouted.

"See the bright moon above?" they mocked. "Get a good long stick and take as much light as you need!"

And all the while to each other they were saying "Christ is risen!" And, "He is risen indeed!"

Stepka turned his back on them. He plodded slowly up the cobbled street toward home. His shoulders drooped. His stomach was as empty as his pockets. Cold and hunger made him dizzy.

That was why he thought he must be seeing things when the row of fires appeared below him on the plain. He rubbed his eyes and looked again. Cossacks! He hurried to get home before they attacked the village.

But, wait! These fires had a certain look to them; they must belong to a band of charcoal-burners camping on the plain. Stepka scrambled down the hill to ask them for a light. Could they treat him worse than his own neighbors had?

The nearer he came to the camp, the brighter burned the fires. Just the sight of them warmed him. The coming and going of people around the flames cheered him onward. The laughter and the calling of one to another made him feel welcome, even though he knew they had not yet seen him.

Stepka walked right up to the nearest fire. He swept off his cap and cried, "Christ is risen!"

"He is risen indeed!" replied one of the men at the fire.

Now this is a proper greeting, thought Stepka. And so he said, "Give me a light for my Easter candles, good people, I pray you."

"Help yourself, and welcome." The charcoal-burner's smile made cracks in the layers of soot around his mouth and eyes.

Stepka reached for the shovel which the stranger held out to him. Then he stopped and stared at his hands. Now that he could have his fire, he had nothing in which to carry it.

"Oh!" Stepka struck his forehead with the heel of his hand. "I never thought to bring my charcoal pot."

"Well, my friend," said the charcoal-burner, "you were anxious for your family. A man who worries does not always have his head on straight." He laughed and pushed the shovel into the fire. "But we can right that soon enough. Spread your coat out over there."

Stepka pulled off his old patched coat and laid it near the fire. His amazement turned to anger as the fellow threw two shovelfuls of blazing wood onto the coat.

"Hallo! Hallo!" Stepka seized his arm. "What are you about, man, to burn my coat this way?"

"Your coat is none the worse for it, my friend," the charcoal-burner told him. "Look and see."

Stepka looked. The fire lay quietly in the hollow of the coat. It never singed a thread of it. Stepka was too surprised to move.

"Good luck to you, my friend." The charcoal-burner stooped to gather up the coat. He handed it to Stepka. "You will have no trouble getting it home. Trust me."

Like a man in a dream, Stepka climbed back up the hill. From time to time he stopped to stare into the glowing wood. He held the coat closer to his face to feel the warmth. It was not to be believed. Yet it was true!

He pushed open the door of his cold dark house. He set the coat gently on the scratched top of the wooden table. With fingers that trembled he lighted first one candle, then another. The last candle flickered as if it would die. Then it glowed as bravely as the others. Stepka sighed.

Softly he called to the children. They would still be hungry, but they would have their Easter lights. Their smiles were his reward. They laughed and clapped their hands and threw their arms around him. His surprise had made them forget their hunger.

But in this night of surprises there was yet another surprise for Stepka. One of the children pointed to his coat on the table and shouted.

The coat was full of gold coins.

Stepka hurried over. He took the gold and let it slip through his fingers: more coins than he could count in an hour! He gathered the children to him and fell on his knees. He wept and prayed and laughed and wept some more.

Outside the little house, neighbors passing by had seen the lights and heard the laughter.

"What have they to be merry about?" one of them asked, peering through a window. He saw the heap of gold on the table. He whirled around to the door and shoved it open.

"I say!" demanded this neighbor of Stepka's. He did not take time for the feastday greeting, "Christ is risen." "Where did you get such a fine fortune? My eyes want to blink at the sight of it!"

Stepka was not a man who bore a grudge or sought revenge. He told his neighbor of his visit to the charcoal-burners.

One moment the neighbor was standing in front of Stepka, the next he was dashing down the hill. Other villagers who had crowded into the open doorway to listen, hurried after him. They had not even reached the plain before the whole village came following.

The leader of the charcoal-burners lifted his blackened eyebrows. He was surprised to see so many coming all at once to beg a light. He said nothing, however, except that they should spread their coats out on the ground. He motioned for his followers to heap two shovelfuls of burning wood onto the hollow of each coat.

Up the hill sped the greedy villagers. They crowed to themselves over such easy riches. They told each other how they planned to spend the money.

Suddenly a cry rang out. Another and another. The fire was burning through their heavy coats! Sparks and ashes spilled down their feast-day clothes. Blisters stung their hands.

All that was left of their riches was smoke and a smell like the burning of fifty tar-barrels.

They turned back to shake their fists at the charcoal-burners. Then they stood with their mouths open. Their groans of pain, their shouts of anger, became cries of astonishment.

The strangers were gone. The fires had disappeared. The plain stretched out below, covered with grass and brush.

Nothing more.

The villagers were sore and sorry, but Stepka kept his gold. He became the richest man for miles around. Yet his money did not make a selfish man of him. His door was always open to the poor. And every year, on Easter Eve, he walked up and down along the river. He called to poor folk, one and all, to come and share his Easter meal.

When he died his grandson, also called Stepka, did the same and Stepka his great-grandson as well. This was how, in time, the little village became known as Stepkov. And that was how Stepkov became the most famous village on the Don.

Resurrection and New Life

In celebrating the feast and the season of Easter, we are not only celebrating the resurrection of Jesus to new life, but also resurrection in our own lives. Children become familiar with this movement in their own lives as they recover from situations like the separation and divorce of parents, the death of a grandparent, parent, or friend, the death of a pet, the death of a friendship, recovery from an illness, forgiveness, and healing in relationships.

In the dynamic and graced relationship that exists between the baptized Christian and the risen Christ there is a source of overcoming, healing, beginning anew, and acceptance. Themes of resurrection and new life abound in stories, although at first blush we may not name them as such. One of these stories is "Your Easter," (anonymous), found in *The Sower's Seeds* (Cavanaugh).

A college girl was on a plane flying from Pittsburgh to her home. As she stared out of the plane window down at the green countryside below, her heart was heavy and tears were in her eyes.

She was a student returning home for the Easter holidays. Her first year of college was nearly over and it was a disaster. She was convinced that life no longer held any real meaning for her. Her only ray of happiness lay in the fact that she would soon see the ocean, which she loved dearly.

As the plane touched down on the runway, the girl wondered what kind of Easter vacation was possible after having such a difficult time in college. Her grandmother met her at the gate, and the two of them drove to her home in complete silence. As they pulled into the driveway the girl's only thought was getting to the ocean.

It was well after midnight when she arrived at the beach. What happened next is best described in her own words. She says, "I just sat there in the moonlight watching the waves roll up on the beach. Slowly my disastrous first year passed before my eyes, day by day, week by week, month by month. Then suddenly, the whole experience fell into place. It was over and past. I could forget about it forever; but at the same time, I did not want to forget it.

"The next thing I knew, the sun was rising in the east. As it did I sensed my feelings starting to peak, just as a wave starts to peak before it breaks. That morning I, too, arose!

"It was as though my mind, heart and body were drawing strength from the ocean. All my old goals, dreams and enthusiasm came rushing back stronger than ever. I rose with the sun, got into my car, and headed for home."

After her Easter vacation that girl returned to college, picked up the broken pieces of her year, and fitted them back together again. In the short span of an Easter vacation, that girl died and rose again. For the first time in her life she understood the practical meaning of Easter.

Another story of life following death is "Great Value in Disaster," (anonymous), in *Fresh Packet of Sower's Seeds* (Cavanaugh).

Thomas Edison's laboratory was virtually destroyed by fire in December, 1914. Although the damage exceeded two million dollars, the buildings were only insured for $238,000 because they were made of concrete and thought to be fireproof. Much of the work of Edison's life went up in spectacular flames that December night.

At the height of the fire, Edison's fourteen-year-old son, Charles, frantically searched for his father among the smoke and debris. He finally found him, calmly watching the scene, his face glowing in the reflection, his white hair blowing in the wind.

"My heart ached for him," said Charles. "He was sixty-seven—no longer a young man—and everything was going up in flames. When he saw me, he shouted, 'Charles, where's your mother?' When I told him I didn't know, he said, 'Find her. Bring her here. She will never see anything like this as long as she lives.'"

The next morning, Edison looked at the ruins and declared, "There is great value in disaster. All our mistakes are burned up. Thank God, we can start anew."

Three weeks after the fire, Edison managed to deliver the first phonograph.

Resurrection Stories in Children's Literature

Am I Blue? Coming Out of the Silence, edited by Marion Dane Bauer. This book contains sixteen original stories of children and young people coming out of the silence of growing up gay or lesbian, or with gay or lesbian friends or parents.

Since Dad Left, by Caroline Binch. A young boy struggles to forgive his Dad after his parents don't live together anymore.

One April Morning, by Nancy Lamb. In this book fifty Oklahoma city children talk about the April 1995 terrorist explosion of the Alfred P. Murrah Federal Building in Oklahoma City and its aftermath: their initial shock and fear, their subsequent feelings of guilt and anger, and ultimately their sense of hope and healing.

The Heavenly Village, by Cynthia Rylant. This is an unusually playful and imaginative story that deals with the mystery of life after death.

The Whispering Cloth, by Peggy Dietz Shea. This is a story of a child who gradually stitches a pa'ndau, an embroidered story cloth, which helps her to relive and own her whole story as a refugee, the loss of her parents, her rescue by her grandmother and her new life.

Allison, by Allen Say. When she notices that she doesn't look like her parents, a child discovers that she is not their child. This hurts and angers her. Finally, with the help of a stray cat that she befriends and that her parents let her keep, she owns her adoption and her family.

Helping Children Enter into the Mystery of Easter

• Give children opportunities to write and tell their own "resurrection" stories as a way for them to get in touch with that mysterious rhythm that flows through all of life.

• Color eggs with the children and tell or

read stories together about Easter eggs.

• Have them interview their parents and grandparents about family Easter customs and share them with the other children. Or invite parents and/or grandparents to come to class and share the Easter customs and rituals that are part of the family's history.

• With the children, read the story of the Resurrection from a children's Bible, e.g., *The Children's Illustrated Bible*, by Selina Hastings.

For Your Reflection & Response

• Spend some time thinking about Easter. What does it mean to you? How do you celebrate it? How or do you participate in the Holy Week services? What are some resurrection stories in your life?

• Read over the resurrection story in the gospels. Pray to the risen Christ that his life in you becomes more and more operative.

• Talk with other members of your faculty and staff about ways of celebrating Easter with the children and young people in your parish.

13

Jesus Is Central to Our Lives as Christians

It is amazing how often over the past few years Jesus has made the cover of secular magazines, like *U.S. News and World Report*, *Life*, *Time*, and *Newsweek* (three times each). Without a doubt Jesus is important to human history and to the world. He is known and respected not only by Catholic Christians but also by people of other religious traditions.

We revere and honor Jesus because he is central to our lives as Christians. Janaan tells a story about how her grandmother taught her the deepest part of what she knows and believes about Jesus. The year she was seven, Janaan was sent to Cascade, a small town in Iowa, to live with one of her uncles, his wife, and her grandmother. There she attended the parochial school in order to prepare for First Communion.

Janaan's uncle and aunt, who had never had children, merely tolerated her. They were not used to having a child underfoot, and so the situation was hard for both them and Janaan.

But her grandmother loved having her around. Occasionally she would come into Janaan's bedroom to tuck her in and tell her stories. Once in awhile she would tell Janaan how proud she was of her because of something that she had done. Her grandmother would say, "You are like Jesus!" Janaan would fall asleep savoring what her grandmother had said. She knows now that her grandmother was responsible for her good sense of self and the loving relationship she has with Jesus. In a simple and prayerful way her grandmother saw the divine operating in Janaan and affirmed it.

That is how we would like children to own Jesus in their lives. Jesus is a person totally unto himself, but he is also made present in people who do the loving thing. It is not only Jesus who is both human and divine. Each of us is, too, and stories can help to get into the heart of that mystery. One example is "The Great Stone Face," by Nathaniel Hawthorne, from *More Sower's Seeds* (Cavanaugh).

In a pleasant, sunny valley surrounded by lofty mountains, lived a boy named Ernest. On the side of one of the mountains, in bold relief, nature had carved the features of a giant face.

From the steps of his cottage, the boy used to gaze intently upon the stone face, for his mother had told him that some day a man would come to the valley who would look just like the Great Stone Face. His coming would bring joy and happiness to the entire community.

"Mother," said the boy, "I wish that it could speak, for it looks so kind that its voice must be pleasant. If I were to see a man with such a face, I should love him dearly." So, Ernest continued to gaze at the Great Stone Face for hours at a time.

Several times the rumor spread that the long-looked-for benefactor was coming, but each time when the man arrived the rumor proved to be false. In the meantime, Ernest had grown into manhood, doing good wherever he could. The people in the village loved him. Everyone was his friend. And as he became an old man, Ernest was still looking for the arrival of the long-expected one.

One day a poet came into the valley. He had heard the prophecy about the Great Stone Face, and at evening, when the sun was setting, he saw Ernest talking to some people. As the last rays of light flooded the massive outlines on the distant mountainside, they fell on Ernest's face. The poet cried aloud, "Behold! Behold! Ernest himself is the likeness of the Great Stone Face."

Then all the people looked, and sure enough, they saw that what the poet said was true. By looking daily at the Great Stone Face, Ernest had become like it. If we gaze intently on Jesus as our teacher and example, we will become more like him.

It's not just a matter of gazing, it's also a matter of acting to free people, to console and bring peace, to feed and clothe, to work to change unjust systems, to share what we have and to give witness to a God of immeasurable love. St. Irenaeus, the great scholar, wrote, "Because of his immeasurable love God became what we are that he might fit us to what he is."

Seeing the Divine in Jesus and in Us

The stories that Jesus told clearly show what a person looks like when they act in a divine way. One of these stories is about a poor widow (Luke 21:1–4). Her story is "The Widow's Treasure," by Christy Kenneally, found in his book, *Miracles and Me:*

The crowd in the courtyard
Flowed in like the tide,
When the priests at first light
Threw the Temple gates wide.

Excited as children they
Ran here and there,
Some came to do business,
And some just to stare.

But others had come
To give honor and praise.
They brought baskets of pigeons
And sacks full of maize.

Then a woman came up
From the back of the crowd,
Her hair full of grey.
She just stood there and bowed.

She said, "Lord, I have nothing,
No treasure to give,
But I'll thank you and praise you

As long as I live,

For your wonderful treasures
Now parted and gone,
For my father, my mother,
My husband and son.

Two coppers are all
I have left in my store,
Here! Take them and welcome.
I wish there was more."

Then Peter looked 'round him
And to his surprise,
Jesus was watching
With tears in his eyes.

He said, "Peter, remember,
As long as you live,
This woman gave more
Than the others could give.

They came with their riches,
Her treasure was small.
They gave what was extra,
This woman gave all."

Jesus told many other stories that show what people look like when the divine is operating in them. Here is another poem titled, "The Lost Sheep," by Christy Kenneally, found in the book *Strings and Things*, that illustrates this point.

Now Jacob had a hundred sheep.
They pastured where the grass was deep.
They chewed the daylight hours away
And at night in the fold they'd stay.

But one small sheep stepped out of line.
He left the other ninety-nine.
While Jacob looked the other way
Just this one little sheep did stray.

His brothers cried, "O brother dear,
You'll come to hurt and harm we fear.

The cliffs are steep and you are small.
O we fear, brother, you may fall."

Their brother never looked behind,
Pretending he just didn't mind.
He'd do the things he wanted to,
So he just disappeared from view.

His head was full of plans and schemes.
He'd climb the hills and swim the streams.
He did not see the cliff-edge go
'Til he fell to the ledge below.

When Jacob found that one was lost
He did not wait to count the cost.
He left the many safe and sound
And he searched 'til the one was found.

He brought him home and made him well.
His friends and neighbors made him tell
His story when his sheep was fed.
"I've found the sheep I lost," he said.

Another of Jesus' stories is the parable of the Prodigal and His Brother, also known as the Prodigal Son or the Lost Son (Luke 15:11–32). This story is all about total and unconditional forgiveness. Jesus told it to show how totally forgiving God is, and to present a picture of what someone looks like who forgives.

Jesus not only shows us how to be divine by the stories he told, he also models it in his behavior. One of our favorite stories is about Jesus and Zacchaeus, the tax collector (Luke 19:1–10). After a group of third graders heard this story and dramatized it, one of the girls said this about Jesus, with surprise: "He was never too good for anyone. He cared about everybody." It was one of those "ah-hah" moments, not just for her, but for all of us who heard her testimony.

The most enduring truth that the Scriptures record about Jesus is that he cared. He cared about his mother, his family, and the guests at a wedding feast (John 2). He cared about his disciples (John 15), and friends like Mary Magdalen (John 20), Mary, Martha, and Lazarus (John 12). He cared about the sick (Matthew 8, 9; Mark 1, 2; Luke 5), the hungry (Matthew 14; Mark 6; Luke 9; John 6), the fearful (Matthew 8:23–27; Mark 4; Luke 8), sinners (Luke 7:36–50), children (Matthew 19:13–15; Mark 9, 10; Luke 9, 18), and foreigners (Matthew 15).

Children's Bibles

Bringing children together with the story of Jesus is especially easy today because of the many excellent Bible story books that have been published. Never before have there been so many on the market. In one of our local bookstores there is a whole section where Bibles and prayer books for children are displayed. Some of the best are listed here.

The Children's Illustrated Bible, by Selena Hastings.

The D.K. Illustrated Family Bible, by Dr. Claude-Bernard Costecalde.

The Doubleday Illustrated Children's Bible, by Sandol Stoddard.

The Beginner's Bible, by Karyn Henley.

Children of Color Storybook Bible, by Victor Hogan.

The Bible: A People Listen to God, by Joan Baro i Cerqueda.

Tomie de Paola's Book of Bible Stories.

The Parables of Jesus, by Tomie de Paola.

Tell Me the Bible, by Joelle Chabert, François Mourvillier, and Letizia Galli.

The Kingfisher Children's Bible, by Ann Pilling.

Let My People Go, by Patricia and Frederick McKissack.

The Rhyme Bible, by L. J. Sattgast.

Bible stories in rhyme have been around for a long time and are popular with children. The Arch Books series, retellings of single Bible stories, are quite successful. Among the many that we like and have used with children are *Amrah and the Living Water*, by Anne Jennings; *Eight Bags of Gold* and *The Rich Fool*, both by Janice Kramer; and *The Boy Who Gave His Lunch Away*, by Dave Hill.

We recommend giving children Bibles as gifts for sacramental occasions and suggest that the Bible be placed on a child's pillow. At night before sleep, children might be encouraged to read stories from it on their own or with an adult.

The story of Jesus is also in the story of people, and children's literature is a rich resource of these stories. Here are some examples.

Twenty and Ten, by Claire Huchet Bishop. Twenty French children, with the help of a nun, courageously hide and protect ten Jewish children.

The Wednesday Surprise, by Eve Bunting. A little girl lovingly teaches her grandmother to read as a birthday surprise for her father.

The Legend of the Bluebonnet, by Tomie de Paola. A little Indian girl gives up her most prized possession so that rain will fall and save her people.

Brothers, by Florence B. Freedman. Two brothers secretly sacrifice for each other.

The Cherry Tree, by Daisaku Ikeda. Two children help an old man care for a cherry tree that has not bloomed for years. When it finally blossoms anew it creates hope in a community.

Louie, by Ezra Jack Keats. Louie, a little boy who doesn't talk, becomes so fascinated by a puppet in a show that he begins to speak. But when the puppet goes home Louie is lonelier than ever until the "puppeteers" devise a way to give him the beloved puppet.

Grandmother Bryant's Pocket, by Jacqueline Briggs Martin. A child gradually heals because of the constant and loving care of her grandparents.

Island of the Blue Dolphin, by Scott O'Dell. A child heroically stays behind on an island so that her brother will not be alone.

An Angel for Solomon Singer, by Cynthia Rylant. A waiter in a restaurant brings happiness to an old and lonely man by treating him with genuine care and respect.

The Story of the Jumping Mouse, by John Steptoe. A little mouse makes great sacrifices to help others he meets along the way.

The Seeing Stick, by Jane Yolen. A mysterious old man helps a little blind princess to "see" not with her eyes, but with her fingers and, more significantly, with her heart.

A Final Word

To end this chapter and this book we're adding one more story as a gift—one that almost perfectly describes the "Jesus story" as it might be and perhaps needs to be lived out in today's world. It is "The Care Collector," by Leo Remington, in *More Sower's Seeds* (Cavanaugh).

> In a bustling village, somewhere and sometime, there was a town square surrounded by trees where the collectors gathered. These were people who made a living collecting things other people had discarded. The collectors discovered that once you had enough of various discarded items, they became valuable again. The people of the village had the notion that if something was for sale, it must be worth buying. However strange this may seem, it was what the people thought, and this notion served the collectors well.
>
> One collector had a splendid supply of glass bottles. He attracted attention to them by hanging some from a tree and clinking them with sticks to make music. Another collector had a cartload of odd-sized shoes. She often commented how odd in size and shape people's feet were, so sooner or later her odd assortment of shoes would be distributed to the appropriate feet. There were pot and pan collectors, stamp and book collectors, golf club and hat collectors, and comic book and sports card collectors. All in all, it was quite a collection of collectors.
>
> One day an old man came wandering into the village asking where the collectors' plaza was located. He carried a large pack, but didn't seem to be burdened by its weight. Eventually, he found the square where the collectors collected, and he established himself off in one corner.
>
> Naturally, the collectors discovered there was a new collector in town, and they eagerly inquired about what he had in the pack. He simply told them there was nothing in it but his lunch and a raincoat in case it rained. "You mean, you don't have a collection of some kind?" they asked. "Aren't you a collector?"
>
> "Oh, yes," he said, "I'm very much a collector. But what I collect does not fit in a pack or a box. I collect people's cares."
>
> This was a strange idea to the people who heard this, so they asked him to explain. "Well, you see, I discovered long ago that one of the things everybody has too many of, and constantly tries to get rid of, are cares, trials, burdens, sorrows, difficult times—all kinds of things that weigh them down and make their lives sad. So I offer to collect these cares from the people and they feel better. Isn't that

simple?"

Some of the regular collectors who heard this thought it was a silly belief and possibly one that was dangerous to their honored profession. They even considered reporting him to the collector inspector.

The old man didn't seem to harm anyone, though, so they left him alone. Soon enough, someone asked him how he collected cares, and he replied, "Well, there is probably something in your life that bothers you right now—some care that you have. Just tell me about it and I will add it to my collection."

"But how will that help me?" the inquirer asked. "Can you make the problem go away just because I tell you about it?"

"No," the care-collector replied, "but you will feel better about it. Try it."

So the person told the old man about something that was a problem. When the story was finished, the care-collector nodded his head deeply a few times, and then put his hands together as if to scoop up something heavy. He pretended to put it in his pack. "There, I have put it away. How do you feel?" he asked.

The person who had the care collected said, "Why, I do feel better. I think I can handle the problem much better now. It really works!"

Word spread. Soon there was a throng of people who came to give their cares to the care-collector. His spot eventually became the most popular one in the square.

One day a woman came into the village walking very slowly and with considerable difficulty. She seemed so burdened that the villagers took her straight to the care-collector. When he explained to her what kind of collector he was, she began to wail, "Oh, you don't know how many cares and burdens and wounds there are in the world. I have just come from a city where there are more hurts and cares than anywhere else. Everyone suffers and no one has any hope left. The worst part is that the rulers of the city thrive and prosper on the cares of the common people. It is a horrible, desperate place. I just had to leave. It was the only hope I had left," she concluded.

The care-collector looked very solemn. He stood up and lifted his pack in a gesture that was slower and more painful than anyone had ever seen before. After a long silence, he spoke slowly. "I must go there."

The villagers and the woman put up a great protest. They didn't want to lose their care-collector. They were afraid that this city might be too much for him. They begged him to stay.

The old man slipped away in the middle of the night because he didn't want his departure to be a burden and a sorrow for the people he had helped.

It was not long thereafter when a weary and burdened young man came into the village. The people knew without asking that he'd come from the city. They helped him as best they could, and when he was feeling better, they asked him if he knew about the old man who had left for the city several weeks ago.

"Know him!" the youth replied. "Why the whole city has been talking about him. Haven't you heard?"

"Why, no," the people chorused back, "Tell us what happened."

"This old man came quietly into the

city and nobody noticed him, at first," the youth recounted. "Then once in a while you could see him talking to people—mostly listening, really. When a person finished talking to him, he bowed his head and did a funny thing with his hands and the person began to feel better."

"For the first time in a long while," the young man continued, "people in the city began to feel better and have a bit of hope for their own lives."

"Yes, we know. He did that here, too," replied the villagers.

"Well, it didn't take long for the authorities to notice him. They told him to leave and to stop meddling in other people's lives. He simply refused," said the youth from the city.

The young man's eyes became very sad and he sobbed softly in his throat. He continued, "They put him in jail, first, but even there he collected the cares of the other prisoners. Finally, the rulers decided that he was a subversive threat to their system of order and control. So they had him executed."

The villagers gasped. Some began to cry.

"I am so sorry to bring you this sad news about your friend," said the youth. "He was my friend also. He genuinely cared about me."

The youth went on. "I feel better for telling you, painful as it is for us all. You know, it is like what he did before he died, his listening and collecting cares." His voice trailed off as an idea began to lighten his burden.

"It still works!" he exclaimed. "Collecting cares still works! You can do it for me, and I can do it for you. He only showed us how!"

The young man jumped up, filled with new energy and strength. "I'm going back to the city!"

"But what will you do there?" asked several villagers in unison. "You'll get hurt again. There are too many cares and burdens in that city."

"Exactly! Exactly!" he continued. "That's why I'm going. I will become a care-collector!"

Bibliography

Anonymous. *Go Ask Alice*. New York: Avon Flare Books, 1982.

Archambault, Martin and John. *Knots on a Counting Rope*. New York: Henry Holt, 1987.

Bang, Molly. *The Paper Crane*. New York: Wm. Morrow & Co., 1987.

Baro i Cerqueda, Joan. *The Bible: A People Listen to God*. Collegeville, MN: The Liturgical Press, 1998.

Barth, Edna. *Lilies, Rabbits and Painted Eggs*. Minneapolis, MN: The Seabury Press, 1970.

Bauer, Marion Dane, ed. *Am I Blue? Coming Out of the Silence*. New York: HarperCollins, 1994.

Bausch, William. *Storytelling: Imagination and Faith*. Mystic, CT: Twenty-Third Publications, 1984.

Beckett, Sr. Wendy. *Meditations on Silence*. New York: DK Publishing, 1995.

Bell, Martin. *The Way of the Wolf*. New York: Ballantine, 1970.

Bennett, William J. *The Book of Virtues*. New York: Simon & Schuster, 1993.

Bennett, William J. *The Book of Virtues for Young People*. Parsippany, NJ: Silver Burdett & Ginn, 1996.

Bennett, William J. *The Children's Book of Heroes*. New York: Simon & Schuster, 1997.

Bennett, William J. *The Children's Book of Virtues*. New York: Simon & Schuster, 1995.

Binch, Caroline. *Since Dad Left*. Brookfield, CT: Millbrook Press, 1998.

Bishop, Claire Huchet. *Twenty and Ten*. New York: Puffin Books, 1978.

Boddy, Marlys. *The Dancing Man*. Boston, MA: Houghton Mifflin, 1998.

Boddy, Marlys. *The Glassmakers of Gurven*. Nashville, TN: Abingdon Press, 1988.

Brown, Marcia. *Stone Soup*. New York: Ch. Scribners Sons, 1947.

Brown, Margaret Wise. *The Runaway Bunny*. New York: Harper & Row, 1977.

Brumbeau, Jeff. *The Quiltmaker's Gift*. Duluth, MN: Pfeifer-Hamilton, Inc., 2000.

Bucholz, Quint. *The Collector of Moments*. New York: Farrar, Straus & Giroux, 1999.

Bunting, Eve. *Terrible Things: An Allegory of the Holocaust*. Philadelphia, PA: Jewish Publication Society, 1989.

Bunting, Eve. *The Wednesday Surprise*. Boston, MA: Clarion Books, 1989.

Burns, Paul. *Butler's Lives of the Saints*, new full edition. Collegeville, MN: The Liturgical Press, 1999.

Canfield, Jack and Mark Victor Hansen. *Chicken Soup for the Soul*. Deerfield, FL: Health Communications, Inc., 1993.

Canfield, Jack et al. *Chicken Soup for the Kid's Soul*. Deerfield, FL: Health Communications, Inc., 1998.

Cavanaugh, Brian. *The Sower's Seeds*. Mahwah, NJ: Paulist Press, 1990.

Cavanaugh, Brian. *More Sower's Seeds: Second Planting*. Mahwah, NJ: Paulist Press, 1992.

Cavanaugh, Brian. *Fresh Packet of Sower's Seeds: Third Planting*. Mahwah, NJ: Paulist Press, 1994.

Cavanaugh, Brian. *Sower's Seeds Aplenty: Fourth Planting*. Mahwah, NJ: Paulist Press, 1996.

Cavanaugh, Brian. *Sower's Seeds of Encouragement: Fifth Planting*. Mahwah, NJ: Paulist Press, 1998.

Cavanaugh, Brian. *Sower's Seeds That Nurture Family Values: Sixth Planting.* Mahwah, NJ: Paulist Press, 2000.

Chabert, Joelle, François Mourvillier, and Letizia Galli. *Tell Me the Bible.* Collegeville, MN: The Liturgical Press, 1991.

Chesterton, G.K. *Orthodoxy.* New York: Doubleday/Image Books, 1959.

Clifton, Lucille. *Everett Anderson's Christmas Coming.* New York: Henry Holt & Co., 1991.

Clifton, Lucille. *Everett Anderson's Nine Months Long.* New York: Henry Holt & Co., 1978.

Clough, Joy. *The Characters Within.* Chicago: ACTA Publications, 1997.

Coles, Robert. *The Story of Ruby Bridges.* New York: Scholastic, Inc., 1995.

Costecalde, Claude-Bernard. *The DK Illustrated Family Bible.* New York: DK Publishing, 1997.

Costello, Gwen. *A Bible Way of the Cross for Children.* Mystic, CT: Twenty-Third Publications, 1988.

Cullen, Lynn. *The Mightiest Heart.* New York: Dial Books for Young Readers, 1998.

Curtis, Jamie Lee. *Tell Me Again About the Night I Was Born.* New York: HarperCollins, 1996.

De Paola, Tomie. *The Baby Sister.* New York: G. P. Putnam's Sons, 1996.

De Paola, Tomie. *The Legend of the Bluebonnet.* New York: G. P. Putnam's Sons, 1983.

De Paola, Tomie. *The Legend of the Persian Carpet.* New York: G. P. Putnam's Sons, 1993.

De Paola, Tomie. *The Night of Las Posadas.* New York: G. P. Putnam's Sons, 1999.

De Paola, Tomie. *The Parables of Jesus.* New York: Holiday House, 1987.

De Paola, Tomie. *Tomie de Paola's Book of Bible Stories.* New York: G. P. Putnam's Sons, 1990.

Demi. *The Empty Pot.* New York: Henry Holt & Co., 1990.

Dues, Greg. *Catholic Customs and Traditions.* Mystic, CT: Twenty-Third Publications, 1992.

Ellsberg, Robert. *All Saints.* New York: The Crossroad Publishing Co., 1999.

Fleming, Virginia. *Be Good to Eddie Lee.* New York: Philomel Books, 1993.

Fowler, Virginia. *Christmas Crafts and Customs Around the World.* New York: Simon & Schuster Books for Young Readers, 1984.

Fox, Mem. *Wilfrid Gordon McDonald Partridge.* Brooklyn, NY: Kane/Miller, 1985.

Fox, Mem. *With Love at Christmas.* Nashville, TN: Abingdon Press, 1989.

Frasier, Debra. *On the Day You Were Born.* San Diego, CA: Harcourt Brace Jovanovich, 1991.

Freedman, Florence B. *Brothers.* New York: Harper & Row, 1985.

Gallagher, Maureen. *The Art of Catechesis.* Mahwah, NJ: Paulist Press, 1998.

Ganeri, Anita. *The Story of Christmas.* New York: DK Publishing, 1995.

Gellman, Marc. *Does God Have a Big Toe? Stories about Stories in the Bible.* New York: HarperCollins, 1989.

Girzone, Joseph F. *What Is God?* New York: Doubleday, 1996.

Gordon, Ruth, ed. *Pierced by a Ray of Sun.* New York: HarperCollins, 1995.

Harris, Maria. *Proclaim Jubilee.* Louisville, KY: Westminster John Knox Press, 1996.

Hastings, Selena. *The Children's Illustrated Bible.* New York: DK Publishing, 1994.

Hazen, Barbara Shook. *Even If I Did Something Awful.* New York: Atheneum, 1984.

Henley, Karyn. *The Beginner's Bible.* Sisters, OR: Questar Publishers, 1989.

Henry, O. *The Gift of the Magi,* (Lizbeth Zwerger). New York: Picture Book Studio, 1982.

Heron, Ann, ed. *Two Teenagers in Twenty: Writings by Gay and Lesbian Youth.* Los Angeles, CA: Alyson Publications, 1995.

Hesse, Karen. *Out of the Dust.* New York: Scholastic Press, 1997.

Hickman, Martha Whitmore. *When Can*

Daddy Come Home? Nashville, TN: Abingdon Press, 1983.

Hill, Dave. *The Boy Who Gave His Lunch Away.* St. Louis, MO: Concordia Publishing House, 1967.

Hoban, Russell. *A Bargain for Frances.* New York: Harper Trophy, 1992.

Hoberman, Mary Ann. *And to Think that We Thought that We'd Never Be Friends.* New York: Crown Publishers, 1999.

Hoffman, Mary. *Amazing Grace.* New York: Dial Books, 1991.

Hogan, Victor. *Children of Color Storybook Bible.* Nashville, TN: Thomas Nelson, 1997.

Hogan. Paula Z. *Will Dad Ever Move Back Home?* Milwaukee, WI: Raintree Children's Books, 1980.

—. *Horn Book Guide, The & The Horn Book Magazine.* The Horn Book, Inc., 56 Roland St., Suite 200, Boston, MA.

Ikeda, Daisaku. *The Cherry Tree.* New York: Alfred A. Knopf, 1991.

Jennings, Anne. *Amrah and the Living Water.* St. Louis, MO: Concordia Publishing House, 1976.

Keats, Ezra Jack. *Louie.* New York: Greenwillow Books, 1975.

Keay, Kathy. *Laughter, Silence, and Shouting.* New York: HarperCollins, 1994.

Kenneally, Christy. *Miracles and Me.* Mahwah, NJ: Paulist Press, 1986.

Kenneally, Christy. *Strings and Things.* Mahwah, NJ: Paulist Press, 1984.

Kielly, Shiela and Sheila Geraghty. *Advent and Lent Activities for Children: Camels, Carols, Crosses, and Crowns.* Mystic, CT: Twenty-Third Publications, 1996.

Kilpatrick, William and Suzanne M. Wolfe. *Books that Build Character.* New York: Touchstone, 1994.

Klein, Lee. *The Best Gift for Mom.* Mahwah, NJ: Paulist Press, 1995.

Klein, Peter. *The Catholic Source Book.* Dubuque, IA: Brown-Roa, 2000.

Kramer, Janice. *Eight Bags of Gold.* St. Louis, MO: Concordia Publishing House, 1964.

Kramer, Janice. *The Rich Fool.* St. Louis, MO: Concordia Publishing House, 1964.

Lamb, Nancy. *One April Morning.* New York: Lothrop, Lee & Shepard, 1996.

Larrick, Nancy, ed. *On City Streets: An Anthology of Poems.* New York: M. Evans and Co., 1968.

Linn, Dennis, Matthew Linn, and Sheila Fabricant Linn. *Healing the Purpose of Your Life.* Mahwah, NJ: Paulist Press, 1999.

Lionni, Leo. *Little Blue and Little Yellow.* New York: Astor-Honor, 1995.

Lionni, Leo. *Swimmy.* New York: Random House, Inc., 1973.

Lionni, Lco. *Tico and the Golden Wings.* New York: Random House, 1990.

Little, Jean. *Hey World, Here I Am!* New York: Harper & Row, 1986.

Lorbiecki, Marybeth. *Sister Anne's Hands.* New York: Dial Books, 1998.

Low, Alice, ed. *The Family Read-aloud Christmas Treasury.* New York: Little, Brown and Company, 1989.

Lucado, Max. *Jacob's Gift.* Nashville, TN: Thomas Nelson, 1998.

Martin, Jacqueline Briggs. *Grandmother Bryant's Pocket.* Boston, MA: Houghton Mifflin, 1996.

Mathis, Sharon Bell. *Sidewalk Story.* New York: Viking, 1971.

Mathis, Sharon Bell. *The Hundred Penny Box.* New York: Viking, 1975.

Maxwell, Cassandre. *Yosef's Gift of Many Colors.* Minneapolis, MN: Augsburg, 1993.

Mayer, Mercer. *Shibumi and the Kitemaker.* Tarrytown, NY: Marshall Cavendish, 1999.

McCann, Catherine. *Time Out in Shekina.* Dublin, Ireland: Eleona Books, 1998.

McCourt, Lisa. *The Braids Girl* (*Chicken Soup for Little Souls* series). Deerfield, FL: Health Communications, Inc., 1998.

McKissack, Patricia and Frederick. *Let My People Go*. New York: Simon & Schuster, 1998.

Mills, Lauren. *The Rag Coat*. New York: Little, Brown & Co., 1991.

Milne, A.A. *The World of Pooh*. New York: E. P. Dutton, 1957.

Moore, Thomas. *Meditations*. New York: HarperCollins, 1994.

Munsch, Robert. *Love You Forever*. Toronto: Firefly Books, 1988.

Naylor, Phyllis Reynolds. *Shiloh*. New York: Bantam, Doubleday Dell, 1992.

O'Dell, Scott. *Island of the Blue Dolphins*. Boston, MA: Houghton Mifflin, 1960.

Pilling, Ann. *The Kingfisher Children's Bible*. Helena, MT: Kingfisher Books, 1993.

Polacco, Patricia. *Mrs. Katz and Tush*. New York: Bantam Books, 1992.

Polacco, Patricia. *Rechenka's Eggs*. New York: Philomel Books, 1988.

Polacco, Patricia. *The Bee Tree*. New York: Philomel Books, 1993.

Polacco, Patricia. *The Trees of the Dancing Goats*. New York: Simon & Schuster, 1996.

Porter, Daniel J. *Shalinar's Song*. Mahwah, NJ: Paulist Press, 1996.

Prelutsky, Jack, ed. *The Random House Book of Poetry for Children*. New York: Random House, 1983.

Quinn, John, ed. *The Loyola Book of Verse*. Chicago: Loyola Press, 1987.

Raschka, Chris. *Yo! Yes?* New York: Orchard Books, 1993.

Revoir, Trudie West. *Legends and Traditions of Christmas*. Valley Forge, PA: Judson Press, 1985.

Rollins, Charlamae Hill, ed. *Christmas Gif': An Anthology of Christmas Poems, Songs, and Stories Written By and About African Americans*. New York: Morrow Junior Books, 1993.

Rylant, Cynthia. *An Angel for Solomon Singer*. New York: Orchard Books, 1992.

Rylant, Cynthia. *The Heavenly Village*. New York: Scholastic, 1999.

Sabuda, Robert. *Saint Valentine*. New York: Atheneum, 1992

Sasso, Sandra Eisenberg. *In God's Name*. Woodstock, VT: Jewish Lights Publishing, 1994.

Sattgast, L.J. *The Rhyme Bible*. Sisters, OR: Questar Publishers, 1996.

Say, Allen. *Allison*. Boston, MA: Houghton Mifflin, 1997.

Seuss, Dr. *Marvin K. Mooney Will You Please Go Now!* New York: Random House, 1972.

Shea, John. *Gospel Light*. New York: The Crossroad Publishing Co., 1998.

Shea, John. *The Hour of the Unexpected*. Allen, TX: Argus Communications, 1977.

Shea, Peggy Dietz. *The Whispering Cloth*. Honesdale, PA: Boyds Mill Press, 1995.

Shepard, Aaron. *The Crystal Heart: A Vietnamese Legend*. New York: Atheneum, 1998.

Silverstein, Shel. *Where the Sidewalk Ends*. New York: Harper & Row, 1974.

Speare, Elizabeth George. *The Witch of Blackbeard Pond*. New York: Bantam Doubleday Dell, 1987.

Spier, Peter. *People*. New York: Doubleday, 1980.

Steptoe, John. *The Story of the Jumping Mouse*. New York: Lothrop, Lee & Shepard, 1987.

Stoddard, Sandol. *The Doubleday Illustrated Children's Bible*. New York: Doubleday, 1983.

Taylor, Theodore. *Maria*. San Diego, CA: Harcourt Brace Jovanovich, 1992.

Taylor, Theodore. *The Cay*. New York: Avon Books, 1970.

Tolstoy, Leo. *Shoemaker Martin*. New York: North-South Books, 1986.

Trelease, Jim. *The Read-aloud Handbook*. New York: Viking Penguin, 1985.

Twork, Carol Camp. *Over 150 Easy-to-use Gospel Plays for Children*. Notre Dame, IN: Ave Maria Press, 1999.

VanWoerkom, Dorothy. *Stepka and the Magic Fire.* St. Louis, MO: Concordia Publishing House, 1974.

Vitale, Barbara Meister. *Unicorns Are Real.* New York: Warner Books, 1982.

Wakefield, Charito Calvachi. *Navidad Latinoamericana/Latin American Christmas.* New York: Latin American Creations Publishing, 1999.

Wild, Margaret and Julie Vivas. *Let the Celebrations Begin.* New York: Orchard Books, 1991.

Wilde, Oscar. *The Selfish Giant.* New York: Simon & Schuster Books For Young Readers, 1984.

Wildsmith, Brian. *A Christmas Story.* New York: Alfred A. Knopf, 1989.

Wilkeshuis, Cornelia. *The Best Gift of All.* Boston, MA: Pauline Books & Media, 1989.

Wojciechowski, Susan. *The Christmas Miracle of Jonathan Toomey.* Cambridge, MA: Candlewick Press, 1995.

Yacowitz, Caryn. *The Jade Stone.* New York: Holiday House, 1992.

Yolen, Jane. *The Seeing Stick.* New York: Thomas Y. Crowell, 1977.

Of Related Interest...

Revised and Expanded
Creative Catechist
A Comprehensive, Illustrated Guide for Training Religion Teachers
Janaan Manternach and Carl J. Pfeifer

A bestseller for over seven years! Covers the why, what, and how of catechesis with essays, questions for reflection and discussion, and creative exercises.

160 pages, $14.95 (order B-06)

I Remember Jesus
Stories to Tell and How to Tell Them
Diane Crehan

The author offers suggestions for making the Scripture stories your own, as well as tips about learning styles, techniques for remembering a story, and more. She provides wonderful stories told from a first person viewpoint, with margin notes that add background and detail, so you can take the stories and reweave them in your own voice, own them in your heart, and tell them with joy to children of all ages.

112 pages, $12.95 (order J-29)

Echo Stories for Children
Celebrating Saints and Seasons in Word and Action
Page McKean Zyromski

Twenty delightful stories involve students (ages 5–11) by inviting them to mirror the teacher's words and actions. Focus on biblical characters and religious and seasonal feasts; includes class discussion questions and a closing prayer.

168 pages, $19.95 (order B-76)

How to Use Stories, Symbols, Songs and Skits for Lively Children's Liturgies
Anne Marie Lee and Elaine Wisdom

A hands-on, highly practical resource with step-by-step directions for getting children (ages 6–11) involved in liturgy preparation. Focuses on the "visual" aspects of children's liturgies, including banners, puppets, collages, costumes, and props (and how to create them).

88 pages, $9.95 (order M-37)

Available at religious bookstores or from:

TWENTY-THIRD PUBLICATIONS
PO BOX 180 • 185 WILLOW STREET ⊗ MYSTIC, CT 06355 • 1-800-321-0411
FAX: 1-800-572-0788 BAYARD E-MAIL: ttpubs@aol.com

Call for a free catalog